THE ULTIMATE HISTORY OF
PORSCHE

This is a Parragon book
This edition published in 2005

Parragon
Queen Street House
4 Queen Street
Bath BA1 1HE, UK

Copyright © Parragon 2002

ISBN: 1-40545-691-4

A copy of the CIP data for this book is available from the British Library upon request.

The rights of Stuart Gallagher and Helen Smith to be identified as the authors of this work have been asserted
in accordance with Section 77 of the Copyright, Designs and Patents Act of 1988.

Printed and bound in China

The authors and publishers have made every reasonable effort to contact all copyright holders. Any errors that
may have occurred are inadvertent and anyone who for any reason has not been contacted is invited to write
to the publishers so that a full acknowledgement may be made in subsequent editions of this work.

Photographic and Picture credits

The GP Library: pages 24 (top), 150, 151, 155 (bottom),165, 171, 173 (bottom), 175, 176 (bottom), 177, 178, 179 (top), 180 (top), 181 (top),
182, 183, 185, 186
Rowan Issac: pages 34, 35 (bottom), 36, 37, 164
Porsche Cars Great Britain: pages 9, 16, 17, 19, 21 (top two), 24 (bottom), 25 (right), 26, 27 (top), 29, 30, 31 (top), 32, 33, 38 (top), 42 (top), 50,
52 (bottom left) 53, 54, 57, 58, 68 (top), 69, 70 (top), 85, 91, 95 (bottom), 97 (bottom), 100, 107, 112, 120, 122, 123 (top), 132, 136, 137 (top),
138, 141 (top), 149, 152 (bottom), 188, 191, 192 and cover image

Other pictures © Neill Bruce's Automobile Photolibrary by:
Tony Bader: pages 123 (bottom), 124 (bottom)
Christian Gozenbach: pages 6, 135, 139
Stefan Lüscher pages 76, 98, 99, 103, 125, 127, 137 (bottom), 140
Peter Ruch: page 45
L. Buehler: pages 80, 81, 82 (top)
Richard Meinert: page 134

All other photographs and pictures © Neill Bruce's Automobile Photolibrary, with the exception of the following, which are manufacturer's press
pictures supplied from The Peter Roberts Collection c/o Neill Bruce: pages 4, 10, 11, 12, 13, 14, 15, 20, 21 (bottom right), 22, 23, 25 (left),
27 (bottom), 92, 102 (bottom), 104, 109, 126, 129, 130, 142, 143, 144, 145, 154, 156 (top), 159, 160, 161 (bottom), 166 (bottom), 167, 170,
172, 174, 179 (bottom), 184 (top), 187

Neill Bruce gives special thanks to Duncan Hamilton Ltd. for making so many superb cars available.

THE ULTIMATE HISTORY OF
PORSCHE

STUART GALLAGHER

WITH

HELEN SMITH

CONTENTS

Behind the wheel of the 2000 911 Turbo

Introduction

'Porsche – there is no substitute.' As a young Tom Cruise uttered those words in the film *Risky Business*, in his guise as a teenager 'borrowing' his father's 928 for the weekend, there must have been many a movie-goer nodding in agreement. For Porsche – or, more precisely, Dr Ing. h.c. F. Porsche AG – is acknowledged worldwide as a name synonymous with speed and desirability; the ultimate sports car. It features on several of the world's fastest and most beautiful road cars, and a number of hugely successful motorsport siblings, and has done for more than 50 years. The German company's prestigious badge remains the wallpaper of choice for impressionable youngsters and the darling of many in the motoring press. More than a century on from its founder's first and much-heralded attempt at automotive design, the Porsche organization that bears his name now sells more cars and makes more racers than ever before, and, with the launch of the new Cayenne cross-country model and promise of a new Carrera GT, the future is looking bright. It's doubtful that even Ferdinand Porsche himself could have imagined how successful his company would become, even with his self-belief and vision.

The story of Porsche is not a simple one. Smart cars are not its only subject: it also covers Porsche, the family; Porsche, the marque; and Porsche, the sports giant; all inextricably linked with those famous models of yesteryear and today. Each model that rolls out of the Porsche factory comes with not only a price tag but also a great deal of history attached. *The Ultimate History of Porsche* peels back these layers to examine each of Porsche's greatest models in detail, including how and why they were developed and how they were received. It looks at the men behind the marque itself; how they triumphed through war and tribulation to create one of the world's most successful motor car manufacturers and race team owners; and how their original technology continues to be used in the twenty-first century in far more than racing cars. *The Ultimate History of Porsche* considers the public's appetite for the road cars; their early and continued popularity among young and old alike; their involvement in all classes of racing and rallying and their pure entertainment value. It looks in detail at the sporting history of this greatest of competitors, from the early victories in the 1950s through the glorious Brumos and Martini years and McLaren-TAG Formula One victories of the mid-1980s, and examines both the many events Porsche made its own, including Le Mans and the Targa Florio, and the many drivers who drove them to victory.

Porsche today is a very different entity from the company of 50 years ago. No longer controlled by the Porsche family, it has occasionally branched out in directions that Ferdinand Porsche himself would never have envisaged or even agreed with. But it continues to make some of the best loved and best-performing sports cars in the world, for road and racetrack alike, and that is something that the great Doctor would never dispute.

chapter
one

The Men
Behind
the
Machines

The story of Porsche is inextricably linked with two men: Ferdinand Porsche, the founder and chief designer of the company, without whom not only would there be no Porsche but few of the early supercars of the 1920s and 30s would have been born; and his son and namesake, known universally as Ferry, who assumed his father's role as soon as he was able, and was responsible for Porsche design between 1950 and the early 1970s, including many of its most famous, successful and desirable models.

Between them, and with the support of a formidable team of engineers, these two men designed, created and raced some of the world's most popular and ground-breaking models for road and track alike – from the very birth of motoring and motorsport through its glory days. It was a battle sometimes – both were even imprisoned for their work at one point – but they strove on to maintain the great name of Porsche in the spirit in which it was created. 'We only make sports cars,' Ferdinand once famously said – and they certainly succeeded at that. Surrounded by a loyal team, they believed in what they created, and it showed.

Eventually, and sadly, the company passed out of the family's hands, but by the time it did so there was little alternative other than to see the great firm go under. Fortunately a return to the traditions of the Porsche name by its board and designers helped restore its greatness towards the end of the twentieth century, and it is today as revered as it ever was. Dr Porsche would be proud.

FERDINAND – THE FIRST PORSCHE

One of the earliest pioneers of the motor car and the motoring lifestyle, Ferdinand Porsche was a visionary in his field. Born in 1875 in Mattersdorf, near Reichenberg (now in the Czech Republic), it was apparent within only a few years that the young Porsche had an astounding aptitude and enthusiasm for mechanical work. Opportunities locally were few, but his reputation spread and by his eighteenth birthday he was on his way to a job in Vienna, Austria, with Bela Egger (later Brown Boveri). Denied any previous technical or engineering training, he found the great city an ideal place to learn, but education was expensive and difficult for a young man of his means to obtain. Nevertheless it was here that he managed to achieve his

Previous page *Father and son. Ferdinand and Ferry Porsche stand proudly together with the first production Porsche, the 356/001.*

Right *Ferdinand Porsche's first design: the Lohner-Porsche electric car of 1901. Presented at the Paris Expo, it won great acclaim for its unique hub-mounted motors and innovative all-wheel-drive design.*

Opposite page
Top *The Austro-Daimler Sascha, a 1.1-litre, four-cylinder model designed by Ferdinand in 1919. Dr Porsche is seen standing behind the car, above the number 46.*
Bottom *Porsche didn't only make cars: here we see the 'Landwehr-Train' of 1912, which was made possible by the all-wheel-drive system he pioneered for Lohner.*

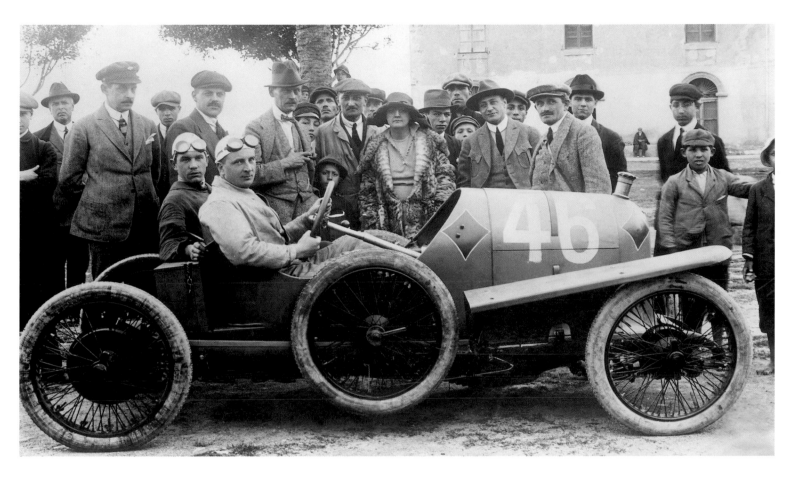

only formal engineering training – night classes at the Technical University which he famously gatecrashed, creeping into the back of the lecture halls and workshops to observe and take notes.

However unorthodox his methods, the experience taught him well. After five years in Vienna, he landed his first job in the automotive field with Jacob Lohner as engineer and test driver, and it was here that his name first came to public attention as an automobile designer. And in no uncertain style: it was at the Paris Expo, or World's Fair, in 1900, that he proudly displayed his first automotive design. Almost five decades before his own company would produce the first Porsche model, the 25-year-old Ferdinand built and demonstrated the Lohner-Porsche electric car. Its hub-mounted electric motors were a remarkable development, praised by the press at the time as an 'epoch-making' innovation. Without gears or driveshafts, the drive mechanism itself could operate without any of the power-sapping friction losses associated with traditional cars. Its lightweight chassis and low centre of gravity suggested sporting use, and a racing version was also planned, which claimed to offer a (for then) lightning-quick top speed of 37mph. Ferdinand's employer recognized the young man's abilities, boasting to the press 'He is very young, but he is a man with a big career before him. You will hear of him again.' And he was not wrong.

By 1901, Ferdinand had delivered one of the Lohner-Porsche all-wheel-drive racing cars to a customer in Luton, England. That very same year Porsche himself, at the age of 26, drove a similar car to victory at the Exelberg rally. So ahead of his time was the design of this motor car that when, many decades later, NASA was designing a lunar car to explore the surface of the moon, they turned to Porsche's original 1900 concept. It seems quite incredible that, over a

Top *The original 'Regenmeister', Rudolf Caracciola, in the Number 1 Porsche-designed Mercedes Type S at the Nürburgring, 1927. He won the race, with team-mates Rosenberger (Number 2) and von Mosch (Number 3) second and third.*

Above *Caracciola takes the win in Mercedes Number 1 at the Nürburgring.*

century later, major motor manufacturers are exploring ways of turning this technology into the driving force behind the next generation of emission-free transport. A reputation for advanced all-wheel-drive technology and performance evolved with Ferdinand and later with his own Porsche company – and continues today.

Onwards and upwards. Six years on from the Paris Expo Ferdinand's genius was becoming well known and he was offered a position as Technical Director to Austro-Daimler, the Austrian end of the Daimler Motor Co. It was a great leap forward for Porsche, allowing him to design and create the automobiles that fascinated him for a large organization that had the budget to build what he suggested. Indeed, he was to work for Daimler in one form or another for more than twenty years, finally becoming Chief Engineer at their (by then Daimler-Benz) worldwide HQ in 1923 and remaining with the company until 1928 – after which he was still often consulted for design work.

He impressed from the very start. From the early days of the twentieth century a series of 'reliability trials' had come about to test the capabilities of new sporting automobiles. Known as the 'Prince Henry Trials' owing to their sponsorship by Prinz Henry of Prussia, they ran throughout what is now Germany, Poland, Hungary and Austria, finishing in Munich. Competition was fierce and the emphasis on reliability soon shifted to speed. It was for this prestigious test that Porsche designed a 95bhp streamlined car for Austro-Daimler – the Model 22/80PS – a revolutionary design featuring four-cylinder overhead camshaft engines and, notably, five inclined valves per cylinder (one inlet and four exhaust) compared with the German Benz team's four. It worked: Porsche's cars took the top three places and the model itself became known as the 'Prince Henry'.

Then World War I intervened and the company concentrated on less exotic equipment to feed the demands of the war machine. Porsche himself continued to impress, though, and in 1916 became the Austrian firm's Managing Director. The next year, he received what he later described as his 'most cherished honour' – an honorary doctorate from Vienna Technical University, the same institution where some 24 years earlier he had sneaked into classes to learn mechanical engineering and draughtsmanship. This degree was designated by the now-famous 'Dr.Ing. h.c.', a moniker which was forever to be part of the professor's persona and eventually part of his firm's name.

In 1923 Ferdinand, whose short and wild temper was legendary, fell out with Austro-Daimler and quit. But within several months he was back with the Daimler organization, this time in Stuttgart as Technical Director to Daimler Motor Co. His early work here earned him a second honorary degree, this time from the Stuttgart Technical University, and he was now universally known as 'Dr Porsche' (and sometimes as 'Professor'). By now his love of racing was well known and a series of intimidating race cars emerged from his designs, including the two-litre, eight-cylinder cars for 1925–7 that scored 21 wins from 27 races for the great 'Regenmeister' Rudolf Caracciola, under the badge of Mercedes-Benz.

Following the 1926 merger of Daimler and the great Benz corporation, further stunning designs followed from Porsche's desk: he was responsible for some of the most sensational motor cars of all time – the Mercedes-Benz K and S series. Offering speed, comfort and prestige to those of more-than-modest means, the great Mercedes-Benz 6.2-litre K, 6.8-litre S, and 7-litre SS, SSK, and SSKL models of the late 1920s were much acclaimed and became phenomenally successful in contemporary motorsport events, dominating racing throughout 1928–30 and capturing the heart and attention of every motorsport enthusiast at the time, whatever his nationality. These fabulous cars were also hard to obtain: only 31 examples of the supercharged SSK were ever produced – the most famous owner probably being Zeppo Marx.

Ferdinand realized that such a narrow market was limited in its scope and that, however much he disliked the idea, car ownership for the masses was the way to go. While he was more concerned with creating the perfect sports model, the demand was for an affordable basic car that the average man could think of buying. It was an idea later championed by Hitler, which led to the development of possibly the most famous Porsche design that did not bear his name, the VW Beetle, but at the time the concept did not grab the bosses at Daimler. When, in 1928, Ferdinand proposed a mass-produced 'light' Daimler, it was considered radical and a step too far for the Daimler-Benz board of directors, who turned it down. Porsche quit the company in disgust.

He then had a brief stay at Steyr, but the economic climate was not good and shortly afterwards the firm collapsed, leaving Ferdinand without a job and at a disadvantage – already aged 55 and with a reputation for stubbornness and wild temper he was hardly the ideal employee, despite his brilliance, and the labour market was full of younger, more conventionally qualified and less volatile men. There were offers, but he insisted on a seat on the board as part of any package, and no one was willing to offer that. But no matter. A phenomenally talented engineer, Porsche was fed up with working for other people – he'd been in the job for almost 30 years but still his pragmatic and visionary ideas were pushed aside. (As his son later noted: 'My

Top The VW Schwimmwagen or Type 166, an amphibious version of the Beetle designed by Porsche and produced in 1942–4.

Middle Adolf Hitler tries out the Beetle while Ferdinand looks on.

Bottom Another Beetle variant, the 1942 Type 155, featuring tracks for use in snow.

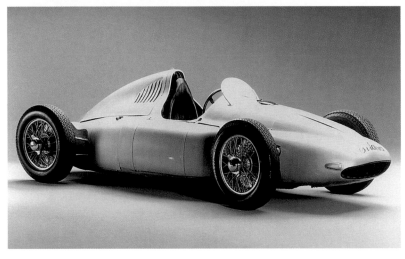

Top *The multiple race winning Auto Union Type C of 1936. Designed by Ferdinand Porsche.*

Bottom *Ferry Porsche's first race design: the Type 360 Cisitalia of 1947. The fee paid by Piero Dusio for this design helped to fund Ferdinand's release from prison.*

father found that when he signed a contract with a firm, they could live another ten years on his designs, but he couldn't.') Ferdinand couldn't stand what we today call the 'corporate culture' of large firms – the personality clashes, bureaucracy and internal power struggles – and he was frustrated that the companies he worked for invariably benefited financially far more than he ever did from his designs. So he decided to go it alone. With financial backing from investors, Porsche Konstruktionburo für Motoren-Fahrzeug-Luftfahrzeug und Wasserfahrzeugbau was established in Stuttgart, Germany, on 6 March 1931. It was a typically bold statement of intent, made as it was against a daunting background of sky-rocketing inflation and worldwide economic recession. But through sheer perseverance, brilliance and technical expertise the company went from strength to strength with Ferdinand at the helm until his death in 1951. There were times when it looked as though he, and the company, wouldn't make it that far though – not least through the repercussions of his work during World War II.

During the five and a half years of war, Porsche, his designers and engineers had no option but to do as they were asked by those in charge of their country. Their talents were put to work designing and building various machines for the military, among them a jeep version of the prototype 'Beetle' (which we shall look at in chapter 2), the Type 60, and the schwimmwagen floating car, Type 166, of 1941. The same could be said for most German firms – and who was going to argue with the powers that were? In addition, Dr Porsche had met Hitler early in the war, but only to try to obtain sponsorship for another of his sporting designs – he was never actively involved with the Nazi machine in spirit but rather saw it as a way to finance the building of a great car. Unlike his son, Ferdinand was simply politically naive; he was totally consumed with engineering, and he did not mix obsession with morality. If there was a sponsor for an engineering project, be it a race car or a tank, he wanted to design and build the best there ever was.

So when the Allies arrived in mid-1945 and asked him to accompany them, it was no great surprise. In November the French invited Dr Porsche to visit them at their occupation headquarters in Baden-Baden. He was apparently asked to redesign the Volkswagen Beetle to be 'more French' and to move production to France as part of 'war reparations'. The offer was probably a sincere one; the French had already nationalized Renault, and had arrested Louis Renault as a Nazi collaborator. But even the French couldn't agree what they wanted: French car manufacturers, led by Jean Pierre Peugeot, wanted no part of a French Volkswagen, and on 15 December Ferdinand, Ferry and Porsche company lawyer Anton Piech (also Ferdinand's son-in-law) were arrested as war criminals. Ferry was released relatively quickly, and returned to work for the family firm, but the others were imprisoned in the ancient Dijon prison without charge. Ferdinand was now 70 years of age and in poor health, and conditions in the prison were terrible.

Finally released at the age of 73, it was only two years before a massive stroke in November 1950 left Ferdinand too sick to move. A few days before, he had celebrated his seventy-fifth birthday and his beloved son had taken him for one last look around the Wolfsburg

Volkswagenwerk, now literally humming full speed with production of the popular VW Beetle that he had designed. He was reported to be entranced and highly delighted. It was his last visit to an engineering plant, and in January 1951 he died.

Above The great Tazio Nuvolari pilots the Auto Union Type C to victory in the Monza Grand Prix of 1937.

'FERRY' – THE SECOND PROFESSOR

The year 1909 perhaps witnessed the unveiling of Ferdinand Porsche's most important non-motorized contribution to the motoring world – his only son. Ferdinand Anton Ernst Porsche was born in Wiener Neustadt, Austria, the second child in the family behind a five-years older sister, Louise (who would also assist the Porsche organization at a critical point in its history, running the show during the incarceration of her father, husband and brother following World War II). The young Porsche's first nickname was 'Ferdy' but, as he recounted 50 years later, his governess did not like the sound of the name and changed it to 'Ferry', actually a nickname for Franz, and the name stuck.

Like his father, Ferry showed mechanical promise from an early age. As soon as he was able, he was behind the wheel of a car and, at the tender age of twelve, was permitted by his father to run in the class-winning Targa Florio entry for Austro-Daimler, the lightweight Sascha (see page 11). He accompanied his father to motor races, even visiting Indianapolis in 1923, and was enthusiastic enough to ask his father for his own, half-sized, two-cylinder car. He

Above *At the Porsche office in Zuffenhausen, Stuttgart, 1950. The company had just returned there following the war. From left: Leopold Jäntschke, Ferry Porsche, Ferdinand Porsche, Emil Soukup.*

spent his formative years playing in and around the Austro-Daimler factory, and when the Porsche family moved to Stuttgart in 1923 owing to Ferdinand's job with Daimler-Benz, the factory and his father's offices within it became Ferry Porsche's second home. As a result he became highly interested in all things automotive, and was remarked upon by factory workers for his close attention and pertinent questions about the manufacturing and engineering processes going on around him, and his interests in the sights and sounds of the factory. Educated in Wiener Neustadt and then Stuttgart, he was reputedly an excellent maths student, and on leaving school at eighteen began an engineeering apprenticeship at Bosch. It was in Stuttgart that Ferry met his wife, Dorothea, the mother of his four sons.

Ferry's father obviously expected him eventually to take on the family business even before his Porsche organization proper was in production: in 1930, Ferry was tutored daily in physics and engineering in preparation for his new role. And it was a good choice, for Ferry would prove to be an engineer and leader to equal his father. Involved with the family organization from its inception, he was to play no small part in the design and construction of many of its early models, notably the Auto Union grand prix cars. He was also the man responsible for most of the test driving, which he conducted with great enthusiasm and little fear – until his father declared one day, 'I have enough drivers, but only one son.'

It was thanks to Ferry and his designing talents that Ferdinand and Anton Piech were released from imprisonment in Dijon. Fortunately Ferry himself had always remained apolitical, realizing early on the likely outcome of the war, so was released within weeks of his arrest and returned to the family firm, which he ran with his sister Louise during his father's absence. The firm was now exiled from Stuttgart to Gmünd in Austria. Ferry kept the remaining staff busy with repair jobs and the construction of simple farm machinery, telling them there were better days to come. And, thanks to him, there were. He worked hard to secure contracts, and it was the Type 360 Cisitalia design that provided the funds to pay his father's and Anton Piech's 'bail' – half a million francs each – and allowed them to return home and to rejoin the organization they had created. Unveiled at the famous Turin Show in 1949, the Cisitalia – designed and built by Ferry for Piero Dusio, as we shall see in chapter 9 – was the first ever race car to feature a mid-mounted engine and four-wheel drive. But he didn't stop there.

It was Ferry's dream to create the first true 'Porsche' model. He wanted it to be a practical but stylish compact car for everyday use, but one which would feature quick acceleration, unrivalled braking and excellent road holding. As he put it: 'If I build a car that gives me satisfaction, then there must be others with the same sort of dreams who would be prepared to buy such a car.' Back in 1939 he had drawn up plans for a car like this based on the Volkswagen that he had helped his father design. This, in 1947, still seemed practical – indeed, Volkswagen were pretty much the only available components at the time. So, in June 1948, was born the first true Porsche legend – the 356 – featuring a tubular spaceframe chassis, aluminium body and a rear-mounted four-cylinder 1131cc Volkswagen engine. The younger Porsche had done well: on his return from prison, Ferdinand reviewed his son's designs and approved of them, commenting to the workers that he would have designed both the 356 and the Cisitalia exactly as Ferry had.

Ferry now led the organization with his father and, following Ferdinand's death, drove it forward to greater things. Between 1951 and his handover of the company in the early 1970s, Ferry worked hard and with diligence to promote and enhance the Porsche marque, not only by the creation of new and ever-improving products but by expanding customer service and product marketing, and of course furthering the organization's exposure in motor racing. He demanded a great deal from his engineers, mechanics, and drivers, but they could see the results. He invested wisely and bravely in new technologies, giving the firm an outstanding reputation as a privately controlled, independent producer of some of the most technologically advanced sports and racing cars in the world. He was proud to watch his son, Butzi, take an interest in design, helping to design models from 1961 onwards, including the fabulous body of the 911 (whose engine was designed by Butzi's cousin, Ferdinand Piech). Eventually Ferry's hold over the company was relinquished as the result of a family squabble, as we shall see, but without Ferry the Porsche of today would be a very different beast.

In 1965, Ferry Porsche, like his father before him, was awarded an Honorary Doctorate by the Technical University of Vienna in recognition of his achievements in so many branches of the automobile world, and in 1984 on his 75th birthday he was awarded the honorary title of 'Professor'. There were many other awards for this most talented and hardworking pioneer of racing style. He died on 27 March 1998 at his home in Zell am See, Austria, at the age of 88.

Above Ferry Porsche stands proudly in front of the latest 356s to roll off the Porsche production line in 1954.

Bottom Some 35 years later, Ferry poses at the wheel of a 911 Speedster to celebrate the great model's 25th anniversary.

chapter
two

How
PORSCHE
Evolved

et us return to 1931, and the beginnings of the great Porsche organization, the brainchild of Ferdinand himself. It was a dismal time to start a business: the disastrous Wall Street Crash of October 1929 had sent shockwaves through business and industry worldwide, bringing bankruptcy to many institutions in central and eastern Europe. All around, corporations were going to the wall and money was scarce, particularly for such luxuries as the motor car. So, to widen its appeal, Ferdinand did not limit his fledgling design company to any particular specialism in the field of transport: the Porsche Engineering Office, based in Stuttgart, was basically a design consultancy that was prepared to take on any project, be it a train, a boat, an aeroplane or, of course, a motor car. They would take whatever they could get, and hope it led on to greater things.

Previous page Fifty years apart: the 1948 356/001 poses in 1998 alongside the latest 911.

Top The Type 32, built for NSU, shown outside Porsche's HQ in Stuttgart in 1933. It was never commercially developed due to lack of funds.

Bottom Ferdinand's first VW designs, the Porsche VW3 (rear) and VW30 (front), were built in Porsche's workshop around 1936 and are shown here outside Ferdinand's own home.

FROM SMALL BEGINNINGS

The first project soon arrived – to design a 2-litre six-cylinder car for Wanderer in Chemnitz. Despite his already noteworthy reputation in the car industry Ferdinand cleverly saw fit to grace the study project with the label 'Porsche Type 7' so as not to give the impression that his small team had no previous experience in this field. And it was a success – so much so that some years later the Auto Union Company, which had taken over Wanderer, would ask Dr Porsche to design a new Grand Prix car because of it.

For all his skill and cleverness, establishing the company was never going to be an easy ride, but Porsche persevered. He knew what it took to build good cars – or boats, trains or airplanes – and surrounded himself with people he knew and trusted: Karl Rabe, the fantastically talented chief engineer, was joined by Erwin Komenda (body design), Karl Frolich (transmissions), Josef Kales (motors), Josef Zahradnik (steering and suspensions), Francis Reimspiess, Han Mickl (aerodynamics), Adolf Rosenberger (business manager), and two relatives, Anton Piech (a lawyer, Ferdinand's son-in-law and later father of Ferdinand Piech, now chairman of Volkswagen), and shortly after, Porsche's own son, Ferry.

Through those early years in the 1930s the infant concern accepted a diverse array of projects, including designing small cars for two different motorcycle makers, Zündapp and NSU. The latter, the Type 32, was a forerunner of what would become the people's car – the Volkswagen. Dr Porsche funded the project with a loan on his life insurance and it was a good investment: the air-cooled, boxer-engined Type 60 known to history as the VW Beetle was one of Ferdinand's most famous designs, a record-breaking German export the Nazis promised to mass-produce for German workers, following Hitler's proclamation that every home needed not only a radio but also a small car or durable tractor. In June of 1934 the Third Reich signed a contract to build prototype Volkswagens, and by the end of 1936 three prototypes had been built in the garages of Dr Porsche's home. In early 1937 further development was recommended, with 30 additional prototypes being built by Daimler-Benz. And the rest is history. The royalty payments to Porsche would continue to underpin the company many years down the line – the Beetle became one of the most famous and loved small cars worldwide, despite its somewhat dubious beginnings, with an enthusiastic fan base that is the envy of many a manufacturer. Although discontinued by VW, it is still in demand and is now manufactured under licence in several parts of Latin America.

But cars for the people were not the passion of Ferdinand Porsche, even though it was this that had led to his resignation from Daimler-Benz.

Involvement with roadgoing vehicles, even extraordinarily successful ones, wasn't a patch on the thrill of participating in motorsport, and it is no surprise that Porsche was also responsible for the monstrously fast and successful Type 22 (later Type C) Auto Union Grand Prix car, the first to use modern mid-engined construction technology successfully.

THE GREAT AUTO UNION PROJECT

As we have seen, Ferdinand was appointed to the project at the request of Auto Union, who had been impressed by his 'Type 7' design for Wanderer some years earlier. Porsche was no doubt pleased to be asked – although it was a move that would later lead to questions over his role in the Nazi war machine and partially contribute to his incarceration.

Left *The office of Ferdinand Porsche in Gmünd/Kärnten. The firm relocated here during World War II. Pictured leaving the factory is a pre-production VW cabriolet.*

Above *Porsche's engineering office has been situated in Spitalwaldstrasse in Zuffenhausen, Stuttgart, since 1938. During the war and for some years later it was occupied by the military.*

Bottom left *The Auto Union Type C, as designed by Ferdinand Porsche. It is pictured here on show at the Goodwood Festival of Speed, where it drew admiring glances from Sir Stirling Moss, amongst others.*

Bottom right *The chassis of the Auto Union Type A (1934–7), designed by Ferdinand Porsche. Its supercharged 45-degree V16 was unique: 6.06 litres giving 520bhp @ 5000rpm and with enormous torque of 630lb/ft @ 2500rpm.*

Hitler had announced a 500,000 RM (US$250,000) subsidy to be given to a German firm that would build and campaign cars in the new 750kg formula. Daimler-Benz and Auto Union both applied and the former won the first round, but Auto Union reapplied and asked Dr Porsche to bring his designs to a meeting with Hitler himself. Due in no small part to Ferdinand's own persuasion, Hitler was convinced, agreeing to split the half-million between the two entrants, and soon the car was under development. Mercedes were not impressed with the cut in their budget, of course, and the result was the great Grand Prix wars of the Silver Arrows, with Mercedes and Auto Union battling for supremacy. The Type 22 was also one of the first cars in which Ferry played an equal design role to his father, in creating both the concept and the race engineering of this winning model.

The Porsches' design, although loosely based on the 1923 Benz Tropfenwagen, was innovative. Its V16 supercharged engine, designed to provide optimum torque at low engine speeds, featured unique single-overhead-camshaft valve control, which Porsche had earlier designed during a lean period in his business. Designed to 6-litre specifications, it would run only as a 4.5 litre with 295bhp. The engine was placed in front of the rear transaxle and just behind the driver (a position now standard for all modern-generation Formula One cars), with two cylinder blocks inclined at an angle of 45 degrees; it was surrounded by a tubular frame and lightweight aluminium skin weighing just 99lb; and made use of differing front and rear suspension systems. The fuel tank sat centrally between the cockpit and the engine, thus minimizing any impact of fuel load on driveability.

The car had unfortunate handling difficulties at first, but its acceleration was unprecedented – a driver could induce wheelspin at 150mph! By 1936, development of the initial model created the full 6-litre, 520 bhp Type C which, in the hands of Bernd Rosemeyer, dominated the Grand Prix season, and brought him the crown of European Champion. They were indeed fearsome race cars, taking everything in their stride, becoming hillclimb champions and setting numerous land speed records.

Right The 1938 Auto Union record-winning car. Bernd Rosemeyer is at the wheel and seems in deep conversation with Dr Porsche.

THE WAR YEARS

The Auto Union project was exciting, but meanwhile the money had to come in, and by 1936 VW prototypes were on trial. Two years later Porsche was overseeing the erection of the first Volkswagen assembly lines in Wolfsburg. The Type 60, the Beetle, was being tweaked and titivated in preparation for series production, but all the while Porsche was also getting closer to achieving his dream of a sports car bearing his own name. As the world teetered on the brink of catastrophe, Porsche and his small, dedicated team were putting the final touches to three exciting cars.

The Type 64 was based on the mechanicals of the Beetle, but with a 1.5-litre engine. Instead of the trademark Erwin Komenda-designed humpback body shell, the Type 64 was clothed in sleek, handsome and aerodynamically efficient aluminium bodywork. It was designed to compete in the Berlin–Rome race, an event manufactured to improve political relationships between Hitler and Mussolini. In the end, though, the Berlin–Rome event never happened: Hitler invaded Poland late in the summer of 1939, Neville Chamberlain announced sadly that Britain was at war with Germany, World War II began and the Type 64 project died a quick death. But even though the Type 64 never ran in anger, its significance cannot be overlooked, for here was the blueprint of the first Porsche. The sleek, good-looking curves, the rear-mounted, horizontally opposed 'Boxer' air-cooled engine, a unique chassis design and impressive performance (it was capable of almost 90mph) – all would, given time, become hallmarks of the marque.

There were other cars, of course – those adaptations of the Beetle for military use – but one could tell that Porsche's heart was never really in them. He longed for the race cars, not jeeps and amphibious people-carriers. But, as in all wars, one produced what was demanded. And he suffered for it in more ways than one.

AFTER THE WAR – FERRY'S FIRST DESIGNS

We have already seen the results of the Porsches' work for the German government: arrest and incarceration in one of France's most renowned and primitive prisons. It's surprising that Ferdinand survived the ordeal, but after 20 months he and Piech were freed in August 1947 after 'bail' of 500,000 francs each was paid by the Porsche family – a direct result of fees paid to Ferry for his design of a new Grand Prix race car. This was the Type 360 Cisitalia, commissioned by Commendatore Piero Dusio, a former Italian champion amateur racing driver and wealthy industrialist, following talks with Ferry himself. Although never raced, it was an influential model.

Ferry had proved his worth, and not only with the Cisitalia. He had also started designing the 356, which would be the first Porsche road car – a car so influential we dedicate the whole next chapter to it. The prototype, like the Grand Prix cars, featured a mid-chassis engine in front of the transaxle, but here used modified Volkswagen drive train components – all that

Above The very rare Porsche Type 60K10 – only three were produced – seen outside Ferdinand Porsche's home in 1939. It is easy to spot the distinctive Porsche styling in this early model, which Dr Porsche reputedly used daily throughout the war.

were available at the time. Ferdinand approved and production began shortly afterwards. The knowledge that he was leaving the firm in good hands and with a viable project must have consoled the old man in the few years he had left. As did the firm's return to Stuttgart in 1950, although it wasn't straightforward: Porsche's original premises in Zuffenhausen were still being utilized by the American military, so initially the company shared workshop space with the coachbuilder Reutter, with whom they signed a contract for 500 of the 356 bodies. This figure, according to Ferdinand, would adequately satisfy world demand for the model. How wrong he was!

Sadly, it was not long after the move that the old man died. But he had lived to see his son's 356 design in production, first at Gmünd and now back at the firm's original stamping ground, and its first major race win: the 1100cc category in the 24 Hours of **Le Mans**. Porsche were on the up.

Top *The 1951 356A of Veuillet and Mouch takes Porsche's first class win at Le Mans.*

Bottom *The gate of the vehicle body manufacturer Reutter in Zuffenhausen, where Porsche shared workshop space on their return to Stuttgart in the early 1950s. Today it is Porsche AG's main gate at 'Porscheplatz 1'.*

PORSCHE WITHOUT DR PORSCHE

Ferdinand's death in 1951 was a blow, naturally, and the end of an era, but the company was safely in the hands of Ferry and would remain so for two decades. It was still only the beginning of the road for the young company, which had already begun what would prove to be an inexorable climb to the very top of its field, penetrating the subconscious of every car enthusiast on the planet. At no stage did it look to be an easy ride, but from humble beginnings, Ferry Porsche and the company he had helped to found persevered.

The initial years were, of course, taken up primarily with the development, and redevelopment, of the phenomenally successful 356. Far from the initial estimate of 500 sales, the model continued to evolve in both road and race form, as we shall see in chapter 3, until eventually production of the final model ended in 1965, one year after its legendary successor – the 911 – arrived and when around 78,000 units had rolled out of the factory doors.

In between, alongside the 400 race victories for the 356 up to 1956, arrived the Porsche 550 Spyder, the first purpose-built sports racer from Porsche, in 1953. Fuhrmann-engined, with a 1.5-litre four-cylinder unit, four gear-driven overhead camshafts and 110bhp, it was immediately entered for Le Mans, and soon became known as the 'shark in the pool of perch' due to its performance, under Richard von Frankenburg and others, in major races where it competed against cars with far more horsepower. It also formed the basis of the popular 356 spinoff, the Carrera, and in its modified version, the 550A, won the Targa Florio in 1956 against tough and experienced opposition. It marked the achievement of Ferdinand's dreams of becoming a manufacturer of race-winning machines; and that was only the start.

GLORY DAYS ON THE TRACK

The next step came in 1957, with the introduction to the motorsport world of the Porsche Type 718. Initially known as the RSK, it had a uniquely configured form of suspension and in its various incarnations was raced both by the factory and its now numerous customers for the next seven years. Its record was outstanding: not just the usual class triumphs, but outright wins at the Targa Florio and the prestigious Sebring 23-hour race in 1960. Dan Gurney, Wolfgang von Trips and Jo Bonnier were just three who learned their trade from it.

By the 1960s, Porsche had taken the racing scene by storm, with their introduction in 1962 to Formula One with the Type 804 giving them their first Grand Prix win. Two years later came the 904; the 906 and 907 not far behind. Soon Porsche were racking up World Rally and hillclimb championships to add to their trophy cabinet. In 1968 came the first win at the 24-hour Daytona race, and in 1969 the first Sports Car World Championship. The 914 was previewed at Frankfurt to great acclaim and it started the 1970s with a bang, winning almost everything in its path.

But was Porsche concentrating on racing to the detriment of its road cars? The public loved to watch, but were they happy with what they were able to buy? Well, they certainly seemed happy enough with the 911. Its basic concept, first known as the 901, had first been demonstrated in 1963, and was available for anyone with the funds to buy one. It suffered dreadful handling problems in its first incarnations, but these were resolved in later models and

Bottom left *1954 Porsche 550, Number 55, as piloted to a class win at the Mexican Carrera Panamericana by Hans Herrmann. It also finished an impressive third overall.*

Below *In 1966, Porsche pioneered the first frontal impact crash safety tests. Conducted at Porsche's HQ in Stuttgart, these involved hoisting a car (here the 906) on a mobile crane before dropping it to the ground.*

Above *Porsche AG's current CEO, Wendelin Wiedeking, pictured in 1998. He has taken the company to new heights, and has recently been rewarded with a new five-year contract, demonstrating the company's and shareholders' faith in his abilities.*

Right *On 16 October 1961 Ferry Porsche turned the first sod in the construction of Porsche's new Research and Development Centre in Weissach.*

there were many of those, including five Carreras up to 1990 and a cheaper model, the Targa, in 1969. 1974 saw the first turbocharged 911, but there were changes afoot at the factory that would lead inevitably to its decline.

FERRY BOWS OUT

Sadly, the family connection with the Porsche firm had been unravelling for some years. Because of bitter personal rivalries between family members and fears of nepotism damaging the health and perhaps even the very fabric of the organization, in 1972 Ferry and other family members took the brave decision, and the right one, to relinquish their hold on the company to avoid undermining day-to-day operations. It was put up for public offering, the running of the company was placed in the hands of key employees, and the roles of the families of Ferry Porsche and his sister Louise Piech were limited to those of shareholders; Ferry, Louise and each of their eight children taking a ten per cent stake apiece. Ferry retained a position as Director of the supervisory board, but it was a far less influential role than he had previously enjoyed. However, he was already in his sixties and the change probably had a more direct effect on the next generation – most of whom had been involved with the factory in one way or another. It was a sad development but a necessary decision, and without it the organization might easily have torn itself apart and been no more.

Initially the new board seemed to lack the direction or spirit of the Porsche philosophy. With the family no longer at the helm, the company seemed to deliberately ignore its founder's famous motto, 'At Porsche, we only build sports cars', by attempting to focus on Grand Tourers and high-volume, low-priced sporty cars. But it appeared that when a Porsche was no

Left *Ferry Porsche visits the Porsche factory at Zuffenhausen in 1991.*

Below *The latest sideline? Triple Olympic champion Georg Hackl holds aloft a racing luge for the 2002 Winter Olympics in Salt Lake City that was designed with input from the Porsche Engineering Group at Weissach.*

longer a Porsche – exclusive, small, sexy and unaffordable by any but the wealthiest – it was no longer attractive. And the sales figures showed it. Despite several new models through the 1970s and 80s, including the 924, 944, and 928, and a massive array of engine/bodystyle options, the company was in trouble. Its now front-engined, liquid-cooled models were seen as inferior to its previous and legendary rear-engined originals; they were sluggish on 0–60 performance by comparison (although still achieving it in under eight seconds for the 928). In 1993 production hit an eighteen-year low point, with only 13,000 vehicles sold. Had it not been for its most famous product, the 911, Porsche might have gone under there and then.

BACK TO THE TOP
In recent years the company has again found solid, continuous and healthy leadership under new Chief Executive Officer Wendelin Wiedeking. It has consolidated, and once again it has grown steadily. With the dropping of the Grand Tourers and the introduction of the new 911 models (initially codenamed 993), Carreras, GT2s, Turbos and the fabulous Boxsters – all featuring leading-edge technological advances – the Porsche product line has once again become the favourite of many a high-flier. Add to that some extremely successful merchandizing, and Porsche is once again a name to be reckoned with.

Now Porsche faces an exciting new chapter to add to its 71-year life with its imminent new model launches. In the twenty-first century the company is still offering world-beating designs, both in terms of its own cars and with models created for other manufacturers – it even optimized a racing luge sled for the 2002 Winter Olympics in Salt Lake City. A recent survey has suggested that along with household names such as Coca-Cola, Porsche is one of the world's most successful and respected brands. As long as that continues to be the case and Porsche continues to build worthy products adored by a wide audience, its continued success seems assured.

The first Porsche

The
356
story

A t the end of World War II, Germany was a shattered nation. Its industrial infrastructure had been wrecked; decimated, defeated and demoralized, the people were shocked and disorientated; and the country was all but bankrupt. Dr Ferdinand and Ferry Porsche were in prison; their Stuttgart headquarters was being used by American forces as a vehicle repair facility and the talented team of workers spent their days fixing farm machinery rather than building motor cars. The future looked bleak.

At least the misery of the war had levelled the playing field. It wasn't just Porsche that would have to drag itself up off its knees – every company would have to fight to do the same. No one had easy successes to look forward to. That the project number 356 appeared on paper a full two months before the Professor's release in August 1947 is testament to the passion and courage of the people who would power the Porsche name into the sports car stratosphere. The 356 would become the first road car to wear the Porsche name and would remain in production for the best part of two decades, with over 78,000 cars being sold, bested only by Project 901 – the 911 to you and me. It would leave Porsche with an excellent reputation and books stuffed to bursting with orders. And all that from the most humble of beginnings.

THE GMÜND CARS: 1948–51

The Porsche team had relocated to a former sawmill at Gmünd in Austria, even though it was far from ideal as a base for sports car production: access by rail was abysmal and the premises were not only too small but pitifully ill-equipped. The German war effort, desperate for materials, especially in the closing months of the war, had led commandeered many pieces of vital production and assembly equipment, and to begin with it was almost impossible to guarantee a supply of components from across the border with Germany. To cap it all, master coachbuilder Friedrich Weber's propensity for a tipple was also known to interfere with smooth production.

These obstacles to progress were coped with, however, and development of the first prototype proceeded. Based on a tubular spaceframe chassis, 356/001 relied almost

Previous page *The first Porsche to bear the name: the classic and elegant 356/001, built at Gmünd.*

Right *The Porsche workshop and auto body shop, a former sawmill in Gmünd, where the 356 was born.*

Opposite page
The 356/001 of Ferry Porsche, shown front and rear (note the stylish interior) and on show as a beloved classic.

exclusively on VW mechanicals, particularly those of the Beetle. The 1131cc engine was mid-mounted, with the gearbox in the back. The single carburettor was replaced with a twin set-up, boosting power from 25 to 40bhp. Clad in a slippery roadster body, the 356/001 was capable of 80mph and, piloted by Ferry Porsche's cousin, it scored a class victory in a road race at Innsbruck just weeks after its debut in June 1948 at the Swiss Grand Prix.

Amazingly, initial planning for the production version of the 356 in hardtop and convertible form was finalized before the prototype was even completed. In place of the spaceframe would be a simple box-section chassis, which would be far cheaper to produce and would provide a structure so rigid and strong that the cars could be driven without the bodywork on. While the coupés were built in Austria, Viennese and Swiss coachbuilders applied the hand-beaten aluminium bodies to the cabriolets. More importantly, the positions of the engine and gearbox were reversed, making the production 356 a rear-engined car.

It wasn't long before Porsche received a much-needed boost to morale and cashflow in the form of its first customer, Swiss car dealer Rupprecht von Senger, who ordered the first four 356s and, better still, signed a contract ensuring a guaranteed supply of VW mechanicals and sheet aluminium from Switzerland. Overall just under 50 Gmünd cars were delivered to customers, each one differing in the details of its construction, depending on customer specification, which makes identification of a particular model nowadays far from simple, even for experts. This would continue to be the case throughout

the 356's life as each subsequent evolution used up the remaining components from the previous model.

The first 'production' models used headlamps from the Beetle. They weren't very effective, but the round lights would remain a Porsche signature. Early models can also be distinguished by the two-piece V-shaped windscreen, which was cheaper to make than a one-piece, curved item. The interior was basic and minimalist, with a painted metal dash and the large rev-counter dead ahead (similar to many later Porsches). A simple three-spoke wheel and floor-hinged pedals were again all similar to the functional Beetle, although the seats could be adjusted and specified as either a bench or independent items. The independent torsion-bar and trailing-arm suspension also came from the VW, along with its brakes, steering and engine, the latter downsized to a 73.5mm bore resulting in a capacity of 1086cc to enable it to compete in 1100cc class motorsport events. Twin Solex carburettors and a revised cylinder head (as of 1949) with larger valves improved the engine's performance to around 40bhp, which was transmitted through the Beetle's non-synchromesh four-speed gearbox.

Add all that to the wind-cheating bodywork and the little Porsche's perfomance was impressive (Ferry Porsche later described the Gmünd models as being able to 'climb mountains like a chamois and touch 80mph easily'), though all in all the cars themselves were pretty crude. There wasn't even a fuel gauge on the dash, which meant the driver had to use a wooden dipstick to test how full the tank was. But despite their lack of sophistication, humble VW underpinnings and relatively high cost, orders for the 356 came in thick and fast. Such was the demand, in fact, that the rudimentary assembly facilities afforded by the Gmünd facility were often unable to cope. In order to improve its production capabilities, Porsche needed to return to Stuttgart. And in 1950, that is what they did.

THE PRE-A: 1950–55

The first official Porsche 356 – the definitive Stuttgart model, as it were – is referred to as the pre-A and was produced between 1950 and 1955. Visually, the pre-A was very similar to the Gmünd cars, the main difference being that the body was made of steel. This was done not just for reasons of cost: the Reutter factory didn't have the facilities to weld aluminium anyway. Body shell and chassis construction followed on from the earlier model, but with many more of the parts produced by machine rather than time-consuming hand-beating. Pre-As were slightly higher-waisted than the Gmünd cars, with a higher bonnet, a more rounded roof and less vertical sides, which allowed for a slightly wider cabin. They retained the two-piece windscreen until 1952, and very few changes occurred during the life of the pre-A save those made to the wings to accommodate the new windscreen design.

The design features frequently changed on the pre-A were the bumpers. The original ones hugged the body and looked very nice, but were inefficient when it came to dissipating impact forces; even low-speed shunts could significantly damage the whole front of the vehicle. The aesthetics of the bumpers changed, and they were moved steadily further away from the bodywork.

The nose of the car carried the Porsche name in silver script, but it wasn't until the alloy handle on the front lid was modified for a second time in 1954 (the first, two years earlier, had added a hole for better grip) that the 356 carried the Porsche badge. The coachbuilders

Above *Cutaway view of the 356 pre-A coupé. Here you can easily see the rear-engined layout that was to become a Porsche hallmark. Note the larger bumpers that help to differentiate it from the Gmünd models.*

Opposite page *Another 356 roadster and a coupé from the Gmünd era. Although only 50 cars were made at the Austrian factory, identification of individual models is almost impossible as they were all developed to customer-specific requirements.*

1953 Porsche 356 pre-A (1500)

Engine
Power unit: flat four-cylinder, air-cooled
Capacity: 1488cc
Location: rear
Valves: four per cylinder
Construction: unknown
Bore x stroke: 80mm x 74mm
Compression ratio: unknown
Fuel system: standard
Power: 55bhp @ 4400rpm
Torque: 77lb/ft
Transmission: four-speed manual, rear-wheel drive

Suspension
Front: double trailing arms, torsion bars, anti-roll bar

Rear: swing axles, torsion bars

Brakes
Front and rear: drums

Wheels
Front and rear: 3.25 x 16in

Tyres
Front and rear: 5.00/16

Dimensions
Length: 3870mm
Wheelbase: 2100mm
Width: 1660mm
Weight: 830kg

Performance
Maximum speed: 91mph
0–60mph: n/a

also had their badges on the front wings (both Reutter and Glåaser, who bodied the cabriolets).

Inside, many of the fixtures and fittings were from the Beetle, but the 356 did evolve slowly. Traditional upholstery in leather, cloth and corduroy became options later. The painted metal dash, with its distinctive central bulge (used to accommodate an optional radio), housed two major dials, a speedo and a clock, although the latter was replaced by a standard rev counter in the spring of 1952. A two-spoke steering wheel with the Porsche emblem on the central horn button became the norm in late 1952, around the same time the gear lever was moved forwards by a hefty 12cm. The cars ran on narrow 3 x 16in pressed steel wheels and crossply tyres, which looked a little weedy but were cheap and strong. Traditionally body-coloured, the wheels became vented and slightly wider in the spring of 1952, reducing unsprung weight and improving brake cooling.

Most 356s today have done away with the Beetle-sourced and fairly pathetic six-volt electrical set-up, which hardly endowed the Porsche with blinding headlamps. The Beetle engine, on the other hand, remained at the heart of the 356's personality. Porsche simply didn't have the funds to set about creating its own powerplant, so instead they set about improving the VW's simple, effective unit. Like the Gmünd cars, the pre-A made do with 40bhp in 1.1-litre guise. The engine was compact and well designed, and at this small capacity there was lots of space in the engine bay to work on it.

The original pre-As had made do with the Beetle's four-speed crash gearbox, but Porsche soon replaced this with a four-speed all-synchro version. The components for this gearbox were built by Getrag, but the boxes were actually assembled by Porsche. The Beetle-style independent torsion-bar and trailing-arm suspension was little altered, with telescopic rear shocks being used in 1951 and a

front anti-roll bar becoming standard fare in 1954. The steering system, too, remained fundamentally untouched, although the brakes were upgraded to Lockheed hydraulic devices in 1950.

However, despite the attraction of the 356's being eligible for 1100cc class racing, and a class victory in its 1951 Le Mans debut, it was clear that customers wanted more power and improved performance. A 1.3-litre engine, with 1286cc, became available as of August 1951. Retaining the original 74mm stroke, the bore was increased to 80mm, and lighter alloy cylinder barrels were used along with chrome-plated, low-friction bores and Mahle pistons to give an output of 44bhp at 4000rpm at a compression ratio of 6.5:1. Later the same year a 1500cc powerplant was unveiled, and with that on board the 356 took third overall in the Rome–Liège–Rome rally. This set-up was made ready for the public by

the spring of 1952. Using bigger Solex carbs, a new camshaft and a roller-bearing crankshaft, it developed 72bhp from 1488cc, endowing the little 356 with 100mph potential. This was predominantly a competition engine, though, but a 55bhp version (doing without the roller-bearing crank) was soon on offer. The star of the range 70bhp 1500S (Super) meant the 356 range now had four models on offer.

The car attracted some stinging criticism for its handling, thought by some to be dangerous and unpredictable, but in truth the rear-engined layout simply called for a different style of driving and talented wheelmen found it both extremely effective and highly rewarding. Sure enough, despite the criticism, that original prediction of Porsche's of sales of 500 was wildly inaccurate. It passed that marker in early 1951, and by the end of the pre-A's production life the tally was fast approaching 10,000. Part of this was due to strong interest from the

Top *The coupé version of the pre-A 356. This 1100cc model formed the basis of Porsche's early racing models.*

Above and opposite page *A 1951 Porsche 356 cabriolet of the pre-A design, beautifully preserved. This car was the first Porsche imported into the UK.*

Above *The last of the pre-As: a 1955 356 cabriolet. Note the Porsche badge that now appears on the front.*

Opposite page and left *A 1954 356 pre-A coupé. Note how the wings have widened slightly; this was to compensate for the new-style one-piece windscreen, introduced to the coupé models in 1952.`*

American market, which had been opened up in 1950. Right-hand-drive variants went on sale in the UK a year later.

Porsche's continued success in competitions also raised the profile of the car among enthusiasts. Crucially, though, the 356 was rapidly evolving: the company listened to customer feedback, learned from motorsport developments and continually sought to improve the car. By the time the engine was comprehensively modified and reworked in 1954 (when the slow-selling 1.1-litre variant was dropped), the car was far more Porsche than VW and every element had been honed to make it one of the world's best-respected sports cars.

THE 356A: 1955–9

The scale of the success of the pre-As was unexpected and very welcome, but Porsche was not about to sit back and rest on those laurels. At the 1955 Frankfurt Motor Show they unveiled a considerably improved 1956 model: the 356A. As was to become typical of Porsche, it was a case of evolution rather than revolution, but that is not to say the 356 didn't become a better machine in every way. It became known as the T1 (thus the pre-As were T0), and evolved into the T2 in September 1957.

Perhaps the most significant change under the engine cover was the introduction of an increased-capacity 1582cc engine. The new line-up of models read like this: the 1300 and 1300S, the latter with the Hirth roller-bearing crank, at 44bhp and 60bhp respectively; and the new 1600 and 1600S at 60bhp and 75bhp. There was also the option of a hot 1500 Carrera. Though the 1600 offered only the same power as the 1300S, it delivered it further down the rev range, and its torquey nature made it easy to drive briskly all of the time. In fact, the normal-engined cars, recognizable by their black-painted fan housings, became known as 'Damen' ('Ladies' or 'Dames') because they were easy-going and well-behaved in nature. Even in Super guises the 356 could easily be used as a town car without overheating, fouling its plugs, or generally misbehaving as certain Italian sports cars were wont to do.

The 1300 engine was dropped from the range at the end of 1957 due to slow demand (a powerful indication of Porsche's desire to react to customers' wishes for more power and

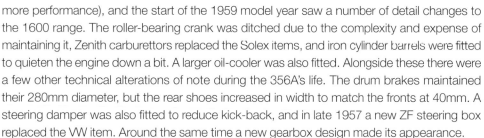

more performance), and the start of the 1959 model year saw a number of detail changes to the 1600 range. The roller-bearing crank was ditched due to the complexity and expense of maintaining it, Zenith carburettors replaced the Solex items, and iron cylinder barrels were fitted to quieten the engine down a bit. A larger oil-cooler was also fitted. Alongside these there were a few other technical alterations of note during the 356A's life. The drum brakes maintained their 280mm diameter, but the rear shoes increased in width to match the fronts at 40mm. A steering damper was also fitted to reduce kick-back, and in late 1957 a new ZF steering box replaced the VW item. Around the same time a new gearbox design made its appearance.

Technical changes aside, the 356A made real progress inside the cabin. New vinyl headlinings were introduced and the seats evolved to become more sporty. The dash became upholstered along its upper edge, the sun visors were padded, speakers were fitted in the footwells, and generally the car assumed an air of ever-greater luxury and refinement. Better visibility, improved pedal siting, gently revised switchgear – Porsche continued to make subtle changes such as these which had the effect of improving the whole ambience and driving experience.

From the outside, the 356A was instantly distinguishable from its predecessors. Wheel size was reduced to fifteen-inch diameter, but width increased for improved traction. The windscreen was no longer V-shaped in order to improve forward visibility, a change which required modifications to the roof and scuttle. The sill was also different, being vertical rather than the pre-A's under-curving style. The rear lights were replaced just before the introduction of the T2, with teardrop-shaped lamps incorporating tail lights, indicator and brake light behind the one lens. The T2 also saw a neat modification that routed the exhaust pipes through the overriders, which had the advantage of neatening the looks and improving ground clearance but meant that owners would have to spend a lot of time cleaning black deposits off the rear brightwork.

Top left Close-up engine detail from the 356S 1600cc model shown opposite.

Above
Top The distinctive rear view of a 1958 356A 1600cc; note the teardrop-shaped lamps. These uniquely incorporated tail lights, indicators and brake lights in one.
Bottom The 356A's cabin was considered stylish and luxurious, as shown in this 1958 model.

Opposite top Assembly of the 356 at the Reutter factory in Stuttgart in the late 1950s.
Opposite bottom A typical 356A 1600cc model, this car rolled out of the factory in 1958, two years into the production run.

THE 356B: 1959–63

The A was another huge success, selling over 20,000 units during its production life, but the desire for new, ever better-performing models continued and Porsche never let up behind the scenes. Even as the A's successor, the inspirationally titled 356B, was breaking cover Porsche were hard at work developing a total replacement for the model.

The 356B appeared to have changed very little from its predecessor, but in fact Porsche had made minor alterations to almost every aspect. It could have been a totally different motor vehicle, design studies featuring twin headlamps being mooted at one point. Typically, though, Porsche opted for conservative evolution rather than radical overhaul. That said, the T5 was still the most radical of the Porsches launched so far. Some people began to say that the 356 had lost a lot of its purity, that it had begun to look a little portly. One of the main causes was the fact that the bumpers were now bigger and stronger. They had also been moved considerably higher up, by nine and a half centimetres at the front and ten and a half at the rear. The headlamps on the 356B were made more vertical, and the front wings were altered to accommodate this. The handle of the front lid was also redesigned, giving the car a subtly different face. Quarterlights became standard fare for the first time since 1950.

The introduction of the T6 variant for the 1962 model year made even more striking changes. The front lid was given a flatter bottom – less pleasing aesthetically speaking, but much more practical for loading luggage. Left-hand-drive cars also got better access to the fuel filler, as it was rerouted through the right-hand wing. Another instantly recognizable change was the introduction of a second bank of louvres on the engine cover. Windscreens fore and

Below Into the Bs: a 1960 example of the powerful and impressive 356B Super 90 – some call it the best Porsche road car ever.

aft became a little bigger too; you could even add as a customer specification an electrically operated sunroof as the 356 began to hit middle-age spread.

One other variation on the theme appeared in 1960. The Karmann hardtop was basically a cabriolet body shell with a hard roof welded permanently in place. Its notchback styling, however, seemed ungainly compared with the factory coupé and it didn't sell well. The interior was pretty much unaltered, with only minor trim specification differences and the switchgear now in black. For the T6 onwards, however, the larger windscreen gave a much brighter, more spacious ambience.

The 356 might have put on a few pounds, but Porsche's engineers always had a few ideas up their sleeves to ensure that the new cars went better than ever. As well as the 60bhp and 75bhp 1600 and 1600S, there was a new Super 90 powerplant with – you guessed it – 90bhp. A higher compression ratio, larger valves and a modified cylinder head were teamed up with improved Solex carbs allied to lightweight cylinders, and this configuration was key to tweaking the extra output from the 1582cc unit. The modifications helped endow the Super 90 with impressive 110mph performance. To help make the most of this extra surge in power, a number of chassis revisions were implemented, principally in the form of a compensating spring at the rear, which helped keep the rear wheels flat during high cornering loads. With the introduction of radial tyres to finally oust the old crossplies, it is little wonder many journalists considered the Super 90 to be the best Porsche road car ever.

Some contemporaries continued to criticise the company for corrupting the purity of the original, but the customers didn't agree. The 356B, just like its forebears, sold very well, shifting almost 31,000 examples during its four-year life. Improved performance, better luxury, exceptional build and longevity were fast becoming part and parcel of the growing Porsche legend.

CONVERTIBLE 'SPECIALS': 1954–62

The 356 prototype was available from the very beginning as both a cabriolet and a drop-top version, and despite what some fanatical purists may say about the removal of the roof signalling the destruction of the essence of a Porsche sports car, the 356's styling suited a convertible body style well and the pretty drop-heads sold with impressive consistency. However, as well as 'stock' versions of each incarnation, some very interesting 'specials' made their way on to the market.

The first of these appeared in 1952 and was known as the America Roadster, named after the country in which the company intended to sell the model. Its aluminium body had sculpted, swooping flanks reminiscent of contemporary Jaguars, with distinctive cutaways in the doors.

Top Dash detail from the 1960 Super 90. The stylish and sporty look is complemented by the Porsche badge on prominent display.

Above An early Carrera: the 1959 GS Carrera cabriolet shown with factory hardtop in place. Note how much heavier this model looks than the pre-A and A models of previous years.

Above Inside the Porsche factory, 1958. Ferry Porsche surveys his workforce as the latest 356s roll off the line.

Below Last of the specials: a 1960 1600cc 356 Roadster, hybrid of the Speedster and Convertible D models of preceding years.

The interior was necessarily spartan to facilitate an easy adaptation to racing specification – few problems were encountered when it came to removing the screen, fitting aluminium seats and stripping away the boot lining to shave those crucial kilograms off the weight to improve performance. Each hand-built example was unique, and only sixteen were produced before the coachbuilder, Heuer, went bust.

The America Roadster had paved the way, though, for the most famous of all the convertible specials, the Speedster. This was introduced in the autumn of 1954 at the request of Porsche's US agent, Max Hoffman. He wanted a lower-cost, stripped-out 356 for the emerging US market to confront head-on offerings from Triumph and Austin Healey. Just like the Roadster, the Speedster was required to be easily adaptable for the racetrack should the customer desire it. The result was a beautiful car with clean, sleek Beutler bodywork and a distinctive humpback. It had a very short windscreen and the hood was rudimentary as it was deemed unnecessary for anything more elaborate in the relatively warmer climes of America. The interior was instantly distinctive when compared to other 356 drop-tops, with its curved binnacle housing the three major dials, and there was a pretty spartan layout in there to keep weight to a minimum, with hip-hugging bucket seats for improved support when racing. Still, the top of the dash was upholstered and the face painted in the body colour.

Engine-wise, the Speedster was offered with both the 1300 and 1300S powerplants as well as the normal 1500. Later, both 60 and 75bhp versions of the 1600 unit would be offered. The ultimate Speedster, however, used the 100bhp quad-cam engine and lightweight body panels from the race-bred Carrera GT, allowing it to power past 60mph in under nine seconds and to top 115mph – a ride almost as heady as the process of writing a cheque and buying one.

In the end, it was a lack of customers that killed the Speedster in 1958. Fewer than five thousand examples were built, and today the Speedster is a cult car, probably the most desirable of all 356s.

Immediately, the Speedster's place was taken by the Drauz-bodied Convertible D. This time the car featured a properly sized windscreen and the interior was much more Porsche-like, with full trimmings. A hardcore of Speedster fans soon voiced their disapproval, though, and with reason. There was no Carrera version of the Convertible D, and there seemed very little point in producing a soft, luxury version of the Speedster when you could opt for a normal factory convertible.

There was one final convertible special, which ran from late 1958 to 1962. It was called the Roadster, but had very little in common with the original America Roadster of 1952; rather, it was a straight evolution of the Speedster and Convertible D. It was originally bodied by Drauz, although after 1959 they were built by the Belgian firm Ancien Établissement d'Iteren Frères SA. Like the Speedster, it sported an unlined hood, but had proper wind-up side windows and bigger front and rear screens, which provided more headroom. There were proper stowage areas in the cabin too, but the Speedster's wonderful bucket seats were replaced by less supportive, more luxurious items. It came with either 60bhp or 75bhp 1600 engines.

Top The stunning and collectible 356 Speedster, one of the most desirable Porsches ever and the best of the 356s by far. This 1955 example has the usual 1500cc engine, but several variants were produced.

Above The America Roadster was designed to expand Porsche's market in the USA. This is a 1953 example, shown in racing trim.

THE 356C: 1963–5

The 901 project, later to become the 911, was already under way when the swansong 356, the C, was launched in 1963. With energies being directed to the new model, development did not progress very far and the 356C remained in production only for a couple of years.

It was still available as a coupé or cabriolet in either 75bhp C or 95bhp SC versions of the 1600 engine. Modified camshaft profiles and larger valves helped carve out a smidgen more power and tractability from the pushrod engines, but in reality they had reached the outer limits of performance without sacrificing the legendary Porsche reliability. It was enough for the SC to boast a top speed of 116mph and the ability to hit 60mph in around thirteen seconds – impressive for the early 1960s, but bear in mind that special versions of run-of-the-mill cars, notably the Lotus Cortina, were approaching these levels for a fraction of the cost.

The 356C benefited from disc brakes all round, at last, but Porsche succumbed to American influences and softened off the ride for greater comfort, using a thicker front anti-roll bar to keep the lurch factor in check. The gearbox and steering continued pretty much unchanged and the simple, functional interior was also carried over almost completely unaltered – in fact, the 356C was very similar to the outgoing B, though the eagle-eyed might have spotted the flatter tops to the hubcaps, designed to accommodate those new disc brakes.

Despite the fact that the C was shortlived and not particularly noteworthy in terms of an advance in technology or design, when considering the impact of the 356 you always come back to that initial prediction of Porsche's in 1950 that a production run of just 500 models would satisfy demand for the new car. It seems scarcely credible that in fact the company made over 76,000 of them, an astonishing production run that lasted the best part of two decades. More remarkable still, despite being replaced by the 911, the heart and soul of the 356 lived on in the skin of the 912, which itself remained in production until 1969. Furthermore, the 912 was resurrected in 1975 to counter the oil crisis of the time, so strictly speaking the 356 wasn't truly laid to rest until 1976.

Below *Last of the 356s: a 1963 SC convertible. Its interior (***top***) differed little from the 356B.*

Above *Engine detail from the 1963 356C SC 1600cc.*

Top left *This 1963 1600cc SC coupé was the sister model to the convertible shown opposite, and was probably created in the same production run.*

The 356 was the car that gave the Porsche name global credibility as a producer of fabulous sports cars. What's more, it gave the company sufficient financial security to develop what would become one of the most desirable, long-lived and successful performance cars ever.

MODEL IN FOCUS: QUAD-CAM CARRERA

The Carrera name is synonymous with Porsche these days. Indeed, the uninitiated can often be heard declaring their admiration for 'Porsche Carreras'. Sadly, the Carrera name-tag has been devalued a little over the years, but that cannot detract from what is a proud heritage. The word *carrera* means 'race' in Spanish, and though now it is applied to the most basic of 911s, when it was first used in the mid-1950s it was reserved only for the most high-performance models.

After racer Hans Herrmann scored a memorable class victory in the gruelling Mexican Carrera Panamericana in 1954, Porsche decided to call the quad-cam engine that had powered Herrmann's 356 the Carrera. The engine itself had come about when Porsche enlisted the talents of engine guru Dr (later Professor) Ernst Fuhrmann to push the 1.5-litre flat-four to its limits. Fuhrmann's design dispensed with the traditional single camshaft and pushrods and used instead two gear-driven overhead cams for each pair of cylinders: one to control the inlet valves, the other to control the exhaust valves. Dry-sumped, utilizing light-alloy and low-friction internals, the engines were incredibly complex to build, requiring up to 120 man-hours per unit, but the results were impressive: the first test registered 112bhp from 1498cc, a potent 74bhp per litre.

Continued success in motorsport proved the engine's ability and durability beyond all doubt, giving the green light for production. In 1955

1955 Porsche 356 Carrera

Engine
Power unit: flat four-cylinder, air-cooled
Capacity: 1468cc
Valves: four per cylinder
Location: rear
Construction: unknown
Bore x stroke: 82.5mm x 74mm
Power: 110bhp @ 6400rpm
Torque: 87lb/ft
Transmission: four-speed manual, rear-wheel drive

Suspension
Front: double trailing arms, torsion bars, anti-roll bar
Rear: swing axles, torsion bars

Brakes
Front and rear: discs

Wheels
Front and rear: 5.60 x 16in

Tyres
Front and rear: 5.90 x 16in

Dimensions
Length: 3950mm
Wheelbase: 2100mm
Width: 1670mm
Weight: 980kg

Performance
Maximum speed: 125mph
0–60mph: 12.8 seconds

Above *Hans Herrmann takes Porsche's first class win at the Carrera Panamericana in a 356. This led to Porsche's adoption of the Carrera name for its quad-cam engine and its most promising race models; a tradition that continues to this day.*

Below *A 1964 Carrera 2. Its famous 2-litre quad-cam engine produced an enviable 130bhp and it would achieve 0–60 in less than ten seconds.*

the 356A 1500 GS, the Carrera, was unveiled at the Frankfurt Motor Show. It was available in coupé and Speedster variants and was soon to be offered in GT specification for those serious about competing. The GT sported lightweight Speedster bucket seats, Perspex windows, no winders, no rear seats and no heater. It had an even more highly tuned version of the 1500 quad-cam putting out 110bhp at a screaming 6400rpm thanks to fine-tuning of the ignition and camshaft timing. The Carreras also used aluminium panels for the doors as well as the front and rear lids to keep weight to an absolute minimum. There were uprated brakes from the 550 Spyder racing car and wider wheels and tyres, allowing the 356's already impressive road-holding to be taken a stage further.

The Carrera not only encouraged hard driving, the health of those complex engines demanded it. Unlike lesser models, the Carrera didn't like being pootled around gently, and if treated in this way would soon signal its discontent by fouling its plugs and destroying those complicated roller-bearing crankshafts.

Despite these unreliability problems (more the fault of the driver than the car), Porsche continued developing the engine and by the end of 1958 there was a bored-out 1600 version with a more run-of-the-mill plain-bearing crank. It was still capable of revving to 6500rpm and producing 105bhp, though the introduction of a second oil cooler seemed prudent.

The Carrera didn't sell that well, much to Porsche's disappointment. They were noisy and tiring to drive compared to other 356s, and because of their higher powerbands they had to be driven very hard in order to extract their full potential. Although by the end of the 1950s the Carrera had 115bhp, the new 356B Super 90 was a more popular option – almost as quick and much more co-operative when it came to extracting the full performance.

Above *The sporty Carrera GS engine, which produced 140bhp and several race wins for the Stuttgart factory.*

Left *Another well-preserved example of the Carrera 2, this time from 1963.*

Below *A very rare 356B GTL Abarth Carrera of 1960, shown here at a historic racing event in Germany. Only twenty were produced.*

It didn't stop Porsche going on to produce the Carrera 2 in 1962, however, with a stonking 130bhp 2-litre version of the quad-cam engine. It was easily able to top 120mph and had a 0–60mph time of well under ten seconds. Even more extreme competition-orientated GS and GT versions were also produced, with 140 and 155bhp respectively.

The title of 'ultimate Carrera', though, must go to the extremely rare Abarth Carrera. Only about twenty of these elegant Zagato-bodied cars were built. They were more aerodynamic, with the option of faired-in headlamp covers, lighter and quicker than the Porsche Carreras, and were designed to race, taking class victories in the Targa Florio and Le Mans 24-Hour, during which one was clocked on the Mulsanne straight at almost 140mph.

The 356 had been raced almost from the time a first prototype turned a wheel, and many parts were proved in racing before they made it to the road cars. The Carrera models took this philosophy a little further: here were road cars that could race. Porsche has become famous for blurring the boundaries between racing and road cars, and these models were the first masters of that art. Ever more extreme, noisy and powerful, the Carrera's evolution took Porsche towards bespoke racing cars, well on the way to becoming one of the most famous marques in world motorsport.

chapter four

A legend is born

The 911

The 911 is the great survivor. In 2002 it entered its thirty-ninth year of production, with worldwide sales fast approaching a cool half million cars. In a shade under four decades it has evolved from a 130bhp six-cylinder air-cooled sports coupé into a water-cooled twin-turbo 420bhp four-wheel-drive supercar. It has dominated in its field and has remained at the top of that field while many competitors have run their course, been replaced by yet another hopeful and been summarily knocked back into line by the Stuttgart master. It has lived through oil crises, economic slumps, automation (until the 1997 model 911 was introduced, the car was very much hand-built), the rise of the Japanese car industry, increasingly stringent emissions and safety legislation and, perhaps of all the threats historically its biggest, the corporate takeover. Furthermore, while the 911's competitors have one by one been taken under the wing of the world's biggest car manufacturers – Ferrari by Fiat, Jaguar and Aston Martin by Ford, Lamborghini by Volkswagen – Porsche has remained fiercely independent.

That the 911 is still on sale today highlights the across-the-board appeal of this sports car with its engine in the wrong place. Even Porsche did not expect the model to stick around for such a long time, introducing the front-engined V8 coupé – the 928 – in 1978 as a replacement for the air-cooled coupé. Just seventeen years later the 928 bowed out of production as the 911 celebrated its thirty-second birthday. The reason for its remarkable longevity is that in today's 911 you quite possibly have the most complete sports car on the open market. Its engine is now water-cooled but still has only six cylinders (while the competition evolved into using eight-, ten-, even twelve-cylinder engines) and is located in the tail; its versatility is huge – you can take your gran to the bingo hall in it with all the ease and convenience of a VW Polo – yet when the mood takes you the 911 is the most accomplished, rewarding and focused driving machine money can buy.

Now that Porsche is in its strongest financial position ever, it is hard to see the 911 not carrying on, continuing to evolve and to revolutionize its market. The competition will continue to attack it, but if its historical track record is anything to go by any successful hits are bound to be nothing more than superficial blows that the 911 and Porsche will take in their stride.

Previous page: The familiar alloys of the 911 Turbo, with their distinctive red brake calipers.

Right Ferdinand Alexander ('Butzi') Porsche, Ferry's son, designer of the 911, at work on an early model of the body shape.

THE EARLY YEARS

Designed by Ferry Porsche's eldest son, Ferdinand Alexander 'Butzi' Porsche, the new sports car from the Stuttgart manufacturer that was unveiled at the 1963 Frankfurt Motor Show was set – little though Porsche or anyone at the show knew – to begin one of the longest journeys in automotive history. This replacement for Ferry's 356 model was initially tagged the 901, but after French manufacturer Peugeot had logged their objections one of the most famous names in motoring history was conceived: the 911.

The new car's simple shape was influenced in terms of style and quality by the 356, but that is where the similarities ended. Ferry had set down a strict set of guidelines which left the design team in no doubt as to where improvements were to be made. The new car needed to be more powerful, to offer better performance, higher levels of refinement and comfort, and in addition to provide more space both in the cabin and storage in order to be hailed as a true GT. The result, though superficially a design which bowed in the direction of the 356, provided the crucial across-the-board improvements that the concept required. The doors were smaller and the glass area larger, to give the illusion of space. The wheelbase was longer by around six inches, not only to accommodate the extra space – although interestingly the new car was narrower than the outgoing 356 – but to provide the basis for the chassis engineers to improve on the car's ride and handling.

Technically, too, the new 911 had taken a big stride away from the 356. There was a new 2-litre horizontally opposed six-cylinder engine, constructed mainly from aluminium in a bid to reduce the weight hung over the car's rear axle, and developed with technology learned at the

Above *The prototype 911, known as the 901. It looks a little boxy compared to the first full production version (see page 53).*

Right Rear views of the 901 prototype. Note the expanses of glass, the narrow tyres, and the discreet engine grilles at bumper level that replaced those which had so dominated the rear of the 356.

Below Ferry Porsche supervises the production of the 911 in 1968 with his son Butzi on the left and and Huschke von Hanstein on the right. One of the first 911 Targas can be seen behind them.

Opposite page A splendid 1964 example of the first production 911.

racetrack, with a dry-sump oil system and an overhead camshaft for both banks of cylinders. Connected to a new five-speed manual transmission, with first gear situated in a dog-leg position, this innovative Porsche coupé came with an impressive set of performance figures. With its six single Solex carburettors in place, the new engine proved to have a significant power advantage over the 356, with a peak power figure of 130bhp at 6100rpm which saw the car reach 131mph flat out and complete the 0–60mph benchmark sprint in 8.5 seconds.

The 911 sported new suspension too. The front saw space-efficient MacPherson struts fitted, which not only secured the space for the golf clubs in the front boot (a laid-down condition for the car's capabilities) but also provided the driver of the latest Porsche with the

responses and feedback expected of such a sports car. At the rear the 356's swing-arm design was replaced by a more sophisticated semi-trailing arm set-up which, it was hoped, would eliminate the sudden oversteer experienced with the 356. The new car also featured new rack-and-pinion steering, and was fitted with disc brakes all round, although the fifteen-inch steel wheels wore tiny tyres just four and a half inches wide.

Just three years into its life, the 911 began to receive the attentions of the development engineers. First, the 2-litre engine was tweaked to produce an additional 30bhp, raising the power to a heady 160bhp. This was achieved by fitting sportier camshafts, larger valves, cleaner cylinder head porting, a higher compression ratio and Weber carburettors. As a result, the 911S added 6mph to the standard car's maximum speed and shaved half a second off its 0–60mph time. The new S also introduced one of the first of many trademark designs for the 911, the five-spoke Fuchs alloy wheel. The S also featured an additional rear anti-roll bar and was fitted with Koni dampers to provide a tauter ride.

Two years after that the 911 began its true journey on the road to greatness. A lengthening of the 911's wheelbase by some 57mm went some way towards curing the car's early handling foible – wild oversteer. At the same time the flat-six engine was further lightened with the use of a magnesium crankcase and the implementation of other costly weight-saving measures in a bid to eliminate the car's rearward weight bias. The car's alloy wheels were also widened to six inches, and the redesign allowed for even wider tyres to be fitted – another concession to providing the 911 with increased levels of grip and handling.

The flat-six engine itself came in for a number of revisions at this

1963 Porsche 911

Engine
Power unit: six-cylinder, horizontally opposed, air-cooled
Capacity: 1991cc
Location: rear
Valves: two valves per cylinder
Construction: aluminium/magnesium
Bore x stroke: 80mm x 66.6mm
Compression ratio: 9.0:1
Fuel system: two triple-choke Solex carburettors
Power: 130bhp @ 6100rpm
Torque: 119lb/ft @ 4200rpm
Transmission: five-speed manual

Suspension
Front: independent MacPherson struts, lower wishbones, torsion bar springs, anti-roll bar
Rear: independent trailing arms, transverse torsion bar springs, telescopic dampers, anti-roll bar

Brakes
Front and rear: un-servoed discs

Wheels
Front and rear: steel, 4.5 x 15in

Tyres
Front and rear: 165 x 15in

Dimensions
Length: 4163mm
Wheelbase: 2211mm
Width: 1610mm
Weight: 1080kg

Performance
Maximum speed: 130mph
0–60mph: 8.5 seconds

Above *The Porsche model line-up of 1972. Left to right: a typical 911 coupé; the neatly-packaged 914/6; a 911 Targa whose Fuchs alloy wheels were fitted as standard.*

Opposite page *A fine example of the legendary 911 Carrera 2.7 RS of 1973.*

time too, with a Bosch mechanical fuel injection system fitted, raising power a further 10bhp to 170bhp, though this specification would not last too long, for in 1970 the 911S flat-six's capacity was increased to 2.2 litres, which again saw power climb by a further 10bhp and the car's maximum speed reach 147mph. The 0–60mph dash was completed in a heady seven seconds. The quest to reduce the car's weight at the rear was also still very much alive, and this time around the five-speed gearbox's casing was manufactured from magnesium. Though these changes were aimed squarely at the top-end 'S' model, the 911T and 911E also benefited from the constant improvements, these 'basic' 911s – if there is such a thing as a basic Porsche 911 – boosted by 125bhp and 155bhp respectively.

For the 1972 model year, the 911S underwent its final and most drastic change. Engine capacity grew yet again to 2.4 litres, and maximum power peaked at 190bhp. A new, stronger transmission was also fitted, and fifth gear was now an option. At this time the 911 also sprouted its first aerodynamic aid when a front lower air dam was fitted, positioned below the front bumper and designed to aid the high-speed stability of this model, the fastest 911 to date. This last 911S saw the new Porsche evolve into a supremely agile sports car. Its light controls, effortless power delivery and keen responses made the car an exhilarating machine to drive.

Below *The Carrera RS proudly displayed its name in attention-grabbing decals along its sides and on the distinctive 'duck-tail' spoiler that graced its rear.*

Bottom right *The clean and compact engine of the 911 Carrera 2.7 RS, which produced its 152mph top speed and the promise of 0–60 in just 5.5 seconds.*

Opposite page *Second generation: a new-style 911 from 1974. Note the front indicators had now dropped down into the new body-coloured bumpers.*

MODEL IN FOCUS: THE CARRERA 2.7 RS

If there is one thing the 1972 2.3-litre 911S did, it was to show that Porsche had only just begun to scratch the surface of the 911's potential. The following year, with the Carrera 2.7 RS, Porsche took its first steps towards demonstrating just how devastating the 911 could be. Conceived out of the need for Porsche to build 500 road car examples in order to satisfy homologation rules and be allowed to compete in Group 4 GT racing, the Carrera 2.7 RS proved such a hit that a total of 1580 were eventually built, albeit in three guises: the RS, a lightweight road model with a stripped-to-the-bone interior; the RS Touring, which featured the interior from the 911S; and finally the RSR, which featured an even bigger engine (2.8 litres), more aggressive aerodynamics, and a rollcage as standard!

It is the RS lightweight that grabs the attention today. Visually it looked special, over and above any 911 that had gone before. With its deeper still front air dam, lipped front and wider rear-wheel arches, and that infamous 'duck-tail' rear spoiler, the RS was true track-car material. It even featured race-car-like graphics, with its red or blue Carrera script running the length of the car's sills.

There was more to the RS than a handful of body enhancements though. All unstressed body panels were constructed from thinner-gauge steel so as to minimize weight, just as the windscreen and rear quarter windows were formed from thinner glass. Even the PVC underseal that had been common on all 911s up to this point was removed, apart from inside the wheel arches. Inside, too, the weight loss programme continued, with light Recaro bucket seats fitted and the rear seats removed altogether. The door panels were also devoid of any excess, making do with simple grab toggles as handles and basic window winders. There wasn't even a sun visor for the passenger, or a clock within the dashboard. The result of these weight-

saving moves was a featherweight 911 that weighed in at a super-lean 975kg, as opposed to the 1050kg at which a standard 911 tipped the scales at the time.

The heart of the Carrera 2.7 RS was its engine. Starting with the 2.4-litre flat-six of the 911S, the engine was bored out to increase capacity to the 2.7 litres from which the model took its name. Both power and torque were increased, to 210bhp and 188lb/ft, and having been fitted with the 911S five-speed gearbox, but with a taller fourth and fifth gear, the RS could manage a maximum speed of 152mph, and could scream to 60mph from a standstill in a scant five and a half seconds.

Gas-filled Bilstein dampers and thicker front and rear anti-roll bars were the only chassis improvements made to the car, though the fitting of nine-inch-wide Fuchs rear alloy wheels (the reason behind the 50mm extra width of the rear arches) ensured the RS not only offered unprecedented levels of grip, but demonstrated the high levels of handling prowess Porsche always knew the 911 had within itself.

Coming straight from driving the regular 911, the Carrera 2.7 RS was a revelation. Its power delivery from the enlarged flat-six was seriously addictive, and still is today, combining the deep-down shove of a bigger-capacity engine with the top-end frenzy normally reserved for peaky sixteen-valve, four-cylinder engines. No matter what the revs or the gear, the Carrera 2.7 RS never failed to produce the goods. Its weight loss transformed the 911's handling too. Already gifted with lightning responses, the Carrera 2.7 RS took the 911 experience to another plane altogether. Its steering was razor sharp, responding to the slightest of inputs while feeding back mountains of information to the driver. It felt so well planted too, and evenly balanced. The feeling that the tail was just seconds from swapping ends with the nose had been eradicated, and the car settled into the quickest curves with the poise and composure of a track-honed racer.

To many enthusiasts, Porsche has only matched the thrills and ability of the Carrera 2.7 RS on two occasions, with the later 964 RS and the water-cooled 996 GT3. Even so, given the opportunity to drive all three examples back to back, it is the original RS that gets the nod. Is it the greatest Porsche ever? There aren't many who would argue that it isn't.

1973 Porsche Carrera 2.7 RS

Engine
Power unit: six-cylinder, horizontally opposed, air-cooled
Capacity: 2678cc
Location: rear
Valves: two valves per cylinder
Construction: aluminium/magnesium
Bore x stroke: 87.5mm x 70.4mm
Compression ratio: 8.5:1
Fuel system: Bosch mechanical injection
Power: 210bhp @ 6300rpm
Torque: 188lb/ft @ 5100rpm
Transmission: five-speed manual

Suspension
Front: independent MacPherson struts, lower wishbones, coil springs, Bilstein dampers, anti-roll bar
Rear: independent trailing arms, torsion bar, Bilstein dampers, anti-roll bar

Brakes
Front and rear: ventilated discs, two-pot calipers

Wheels
Front: Fuchs alloy, 6J x 15in
Rear: Fuchs alloy, 7J x 15in

Tyres
Front: 185/70VR15
Rear: 215/60VR15

Dimensions
Length: 4163mm
Wheelbase: 2268mm
Width: 1610mm
Weight: 975kg

Performance
Maximum speed: 152mph
0–60mph: 5.5 seconds

THE SECOND GENERATION

Following the Carrera 2.7 RS, all 911s produced from 1974 were fitted with the 2.7-litre flat-six engine, albeit in various states of tune ranging from a disappointing 150bhp for the standard car, through 210bhp for the 911 Carrera and a turbocharged 260bhp for the 911 Turbo. Additional changes to the 911 were the result of the need for the car to conform to safety legislation in the United States, which stated that a road car's bumpers should be capable of absorbing an impact of up to 5mph without deformation or causing damage to any part of the car. The solution from Porsche was to blend the new bumpers into the bodywork, allowing the incorporation of unseen hydraulic dampers for the American-market cars. The fitting of these bumpers was the first significant alteration to the 911's shape in its eleven-year history.

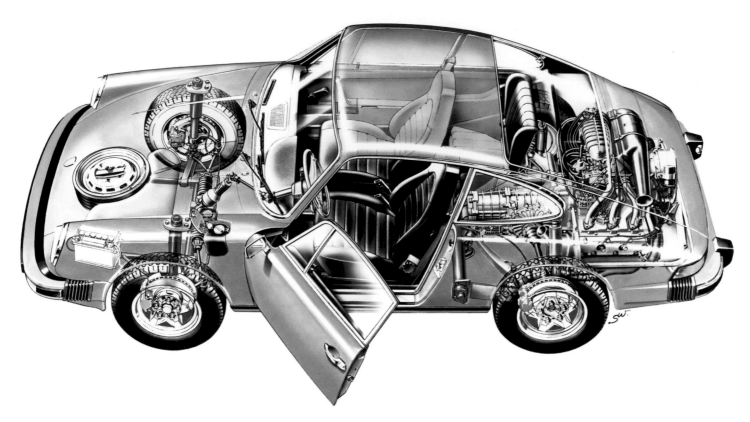

1974 Porsche Carrera 2.7

Engine
Power unit: six-cylinder, horizontally opposed, air-cooled
Capacity: 2687cc
Location: rear
Valves: two valves per cylinder
Construction: aluminium/magnesium
Bore x stroke: 90mm x 70.4mm
Compression ratio: 8.0:1
Fuel system: Bosch K-Jetronic injection
Power: 150bhp @ 5700rpm
Torque: 173lb/ft @ 3800rpm
Transmission: five-speed manual

Suspension
Front: independent MacPherson struts, lower wishbones, torsion bar springs, anti-roll bar
Rear: independent trailing arms, transverse torsion bar springs, telescopic dampers, anti-roll bar

Brakes
Front and rear: ventilated discs, two-pot calipers

Wheels
Front: 5.5J x 15in
Rear: 7J x 15in

Tyres
Front: 185/70VR15
Rear: 215/60VR15

Dimensions
Length: 4291mm
Wheelbase: 2272mm
Width: 1610mm
Weight: 1080kg

Performance
Maximum speed: 130mph
0–60mph: 8.2 seconds

This second generation of 911s also saw the introduction of the firm's infamous 'whale-tail' rear spoiler, introduced to the new Carrera model, which also inherited the 3-litre engine that had been fitted to the original 911 Turbo, albeit without the KKK turbocharger. The fitting of this new engine was a significant step, because it actually saw peak power fall to 200bhp, which was less than the previous 2.7-litre engine due to the ever more stringent emission regulations; influenced by American legislation, they were fast becoming the norm in Europe too. Equipping the 3-litre engine with a Bosch K-Jetronic fuel injection system, however, ensured that performance was at least on par with the smaller unit, a 3-litre car capable of a maximum speed of 150mph and a 6.3-second 0–60mph time.

During the 1970s Porsche continued on a development programme that saw the car's chassis and brakes continuously uprated in order to cope with the car's increased performance. Both the front and rear anti-roll bars became larger, and for the 3-litre Carrera model Bilstein dampers became standard equipment. The biggest change, however, was the move to a forged aluminium alloy semi-trailing arm suspension set-up. Not only did this lower the rear weight even further, it also went some way to ensuring the car became more progressive and controllable as the driver reached its limits. By 1980 the 911 range had been whittled down to just two models: the 911 Turbo, whose capacity had grown to 3.3 litres, and the 3.0SC, which was a combination of the old 2.7-litre and Carrera models, with the 3-litre engine. The 911 model line would run with this configuration until 1984, when the new 911 Carrera was launched.

This page *The new Carrera 2.7 of 1974. This heavier 911 lacked the all-out power and performance of the RS but was still a very impressive car.*

Opposite page *Cutaway of the second generation 911 of 1974*

This page *The first 911 Turbo, originally codenamed the Type 930. Its distinctive flared wheel arches and whale-tail spoiler were required for homologation. Originally priced close to £15,000, the 1975 example pictured was Porsche's UK demonstrator of the model.*

Opposite page *A 1980 example of the 3.3 Turbo, produced from 1978 to 1989.*

MODEL IN FOCUS: 930 TURBO AND 3.3 TURBO

The 911 Turbo *is* the 911. Originally, at the 1974 Paris Motor Show, the 911 Turbo featured a 3-litre flat-six engine with a single KKK turbocharger which pushed power output to a formidable 260bhp at 5500rpm and provided the 911 Turbo with the necessary package to propel it from 0–60 in six seconds and to go on to a 155mph maximum speed. Developed from the 3-litre flat-six engine used in the RSR racer, the turbo unit featured a stronger aluminium crankcase and a lower compression ratio, and the turbocharger was set to run at a maximum 12psi. To cope with this extra power a stronger four-speed gearbox was employed in place of the regular five-speed box, and a larger clutch was used.

The Turbo was intended originally as a homologation special to qualify Porsche for racing in the proposed Group 4 'silhouette racing' formula – Porsche needed to build and sell 400 of these cars by 1976 to be eligible. In fact, demand was so strong for the Turbo that it went on general sale for the 1975 model year and was quickly snapped up. With its infamous 'whale-tail' rear spoiler and flared front and rear arches housing seven- and eight-inch-wide alloy wheels wrapped in sticky Pirelli P7 rubber, the 911 Turbo had landed and was ready to take on all comers. And not just on the road but on the racetrack too: a Turbo won Le Mans in its first year out and its racing derivatives, the 935 and 936, proved unbeatable in the following years at all styles of motorsport, as we shall see in chapter 9.

In 1978, three years after its initial launch, the roadgoing Turbo's engine capacity rose to 3.3 litres, and with that came a power increase

1984 Porsche 911 Turbo (3.3)

Engine
Power unit: six-cylinder, horizontally opposed, air-cooled, single KKK turbocharger
Capacity: 3299cc
Location: rear
Valves: two valves per cylinder
Construction: aluminium/steel
Bore x stroke: 97mm x 74.4mm
Compression ratio: 7.0:1
Fuel system: Bosch K-Jetronic injection
Power: 300bhp @ 5500rpm
Torque: 318lb/ft @ 4000rpm
Transmission: four-speed manual

Suspension
Front: independent MacPherson struts, lower wishbones, coil springs, Bilstein dampers, anti-roll bar
Rear: independent trailing arms, torsion bar, Bilstein dampers, anti-roll bar

Brakes
Front and rear: ventilated discs, four-pot calipers

Wheels
Front: Fuchs alloy, 7J x 16in
Rear: Fuchs alloy, 9J x 16in

Tyres
Front: 205/55VR16
Rear: 245/45VR16

Dimensions
Length: 4293mm
Wheelbase: 2273mm
Width: 1773mm
Weight: 1335kg

Performance
Maximum speed: 160mph
0–60mph: 5.3 seconds

Right How did they fit it all in? The monstrous 3.3 engine of the 1980 911 Turbo was a far cry from the old VW days.

1984 Porsche Carrera (3.2)

Engine
Power unit: six-cylinder, horizontally opposed, air-cooled
Capacity: 3164cc
Location: rear
Valves: two valves per cylinder
Construction: aluminium/steel
Bore x stroke: 95mm x 74.4mm
Compression ratio: 10.3:1
Fuel system: Bosch DME programmed injection/ignition
Power: 231bhp @ 5900rpm
Torque: 210lb/ft @ 4800rpm
Transmission: five-speed manual

Suspension
Front: independent MacPherson struts, lower wishbones, coil springs, Bilstein dampers, anti-roll bar
Rear: independent trailing arms, transverse torsion bar springs, Bilstein dampers, anti-roll bar

Brakes
Front and rear: ventilated discs, four-piston calipers

Wheels
Front: 6J x 16in
Rear: 7J x 16in

Tyres
Front: 205/55VR16
Rear: 225/50VR16

Dimensions
Length: 4293mm
Wheelbase: 2273mm
Width: 1651mm
Weight: 1160kg

Performance
Maximum speed: 152mph
0–60mph: 5.3 seconds

to 300bhp. As a result the 911 Turbo's performance statistics were now well into the supercar league, with a 5.3-second 0–60mph time and 160mph as a maximum speed. The 3.3-litre engine was much more than just an increase in bore capacity, though. The stroke was increased along with the bore, the compression raised, and larger bearings and an intercooler for the turbocharger were fitted. More importantly, perhaps, for the enthusiastic driver was the fitting of larger cross-drilled four-piston caliper brakes inherited from the 917 Le Mans race cars. They proved just as popular as the original, with some 10,000 sold worldwide by 1983.

Driving an original 911 Turbo is still an occasion today, even if the first cars are fast approaching their thirtieth anniversary, but, as with all early turbocharged cars, the 911 Turbo suffers from a serious dose of turbo lag – which in layman's terms means you can floor the throttle at, say, 2000rpm in any gear but you'll be waiting until around 4000rpm for the turbocharger to spin up to its maximum revs and catapult you down the road. From the moment you enter the Turbo's sweet spot, though, the fireworks begin. Acceleration is nothing short of mind-blowing. The revs hit the limiter with the violence of a prop forward taking out a fast-approaching opposition wing, and the speed climbs at an unprecedented rate, 10mph increments being added to the speedometer at such a rate of knots you would be forgiven for thinking you were sitting in an aeroplane as it sprinted along the runway for take-off. And there is more to the original 911 Turbos than their raw speed. With its rear-end weight bias and peaky power delivery, the 911 Turbo demands to be driven in a smooth and precise manner. The 911 has never been a car with which you can take liberties, and in the 911 Turbo that level of respect was taken a step further.

NEW MANAGEMENT, NEW MODEL

Following the introduction of the first Carrera models, the 911 had to all intents and purposes gone soft. Development of the model had all but stopped, production of the 911 expected to cease with the introduction in 1981 of the front-engined, water-cooled 944 coupé. But the 911 refused to go quietly, showing the same tenacity in the face of impending discontinuation as it had done a couple of years earlier when the V8-engined 928 (again front-engined and water-cooled) was introduced as a direct replacement and went on to sell only a fraction of the models the 911 had shifted. Change was needed, and fast.

New management was the first move, and Porsche introduced Peter W. Schutz as the new company chairman in place of Dr Ernst Fuhrmann. A dedicated fan of the 911, and backed by Ferry Porsche himself, Schutz quickly reinstated the car in the company's model plans, and the result, in 1984, was the launch of the new 3.2 Carrera. A new 3.2-litre engine producing 231bhp was installed into the new model's tail, which featured many technological developments first seen on the Turbo. Mating the existing alloy block to the Turbo engine's longer-stroke crank provided the extra capacity, while larger valves, manifolds and exhaust system, higher-compression pistons and a new Bosch DME injection and ignition system brought the 911 bang up to date.

With an increase in power and torque (up to 231bhp and 210lb/ft respectively) and fuel consumption, the 911 had been thoroughly revamped. New gear ratios were fitted to optimize the engine's performance, and an oil cooler was also fitted to the gearbox to ensure the sweetest of changes at all times. Thicker brake discs were added to the recipe, and if the Sport Equipment option was selected, stiffer dampers were fitted, as was a rear spoiler and larger alloy wheels with Pirelli P7 tyres.

On paper, the new 3.2 Carrera had returned the 911 to its former glory. Although Porsche claimed it was no faster than the original 2.7 car, with a 152mph maximum speed and 6.1-second 0–60mph (although subsequent magazine road tests reduced this figure to 5.3 seconds), the new 911 was an even sweeter and more rewarding car to drive than the

Below *The new Carrera for the 1980s, with its 3.2 litre engine, borrowed much from the 3.3 Turbo and proved just as attractive to the buyer, rescuing the 911 series from an untimely end.*

Right *The tail of the 1986 3.2 Carrera, showing the famous huge rear spoiler.*

Opposite page *Designated the Porsche 964, the new generation four-wheel-drive Carrera 4 featured smoother body lines and a retractable spoiler for improved aerodynamic performance.*

outgoing model. In a world struggling in the grip of a recession, however, it was not long after the debut of this new model that Porsche, along with its European counterparts, was staring financial obstacles in the face, at the same time having to fend off a determined attack from Japan, whose companies had launched head-on into the sports car market. It was soon evident that the 911 needed yet another overhaul, and quickly.

With the launch of the 959 supercar in 1987 (see chapter 7), Porsche showed it could still lead the field in innovation. Here was a car that featured four-wheel-drive, four-wheel-steer technology. Its twin turbocharged 450bhp flat-six engine could propel the six-speed, composite-clothed machine to a 199mph maximum speed. The factory might not have ended up making much of a profit on these strictly limited machines (some stories even reported that they actually lost money on every car sold), but they stirred a great deal of interest in the marque once again, both in the press and, more crucially, in the dealerships.

THE '964' GENERATION

In 1989 Porsche introduced what many hardcore enthusiasts claim to be the real second-generation 911. With an altered factory designation name – 964 – the updated 911 was 87 per cent new and ready to lead Porsche strongly up the path of recovery.

Visually, the new car was distinctively different, even though it had retained the front boot lid and wings, doors and roof. New moulded bumpers played a bigger role in transforming the still classically recognizable 911 shape, with their smooth, more cohesive contours and their designed-in driving lamps enabling the car's bodyline to flow uninterrupted. Perhaps the biggest influence on how the new car looked, though, was the retractable rear spoiler. Confronted with the dilemma of how to retain the classic 911 shape and at the same time improve the car's aerodynamic performance, not to mention engine cooling, at speed, Porsche housed the rear spoiler in the engine cover, enabling it to rise automatically at 50mph and retract at 6mph. Other aerodynamic changes focused on detail improvements to the 911's general shape. Rain gutters were reduced in size, front and rear windows were fitted flusher to the bodywork, and superfluous body trim was kept to a minimum. In all, the 964 generation was a more cohesive design than had been seen since the days of the original in 1963, and effectively provided Porsche with the tool it required (and could afford) to climb out of the slump it had got itself into.

That this next generation was only originally available with a four-wheel-drive transmission demonstrates just how serious the firm was in establishing the new car as just that – a new 911. The Carrera 4 was launched in 1989 and featured a much simpler four-wheel-drive system to that which had previously been fitted to the 959. Using a standard five-speed gearbox, drive was sent to the front wheel via a central epicyclic differential that split the 911's drive 31 per cent to the front and 69 per cent to the rear. The slip of both the front and rear differentials was controlled by a multi-plate clutch, which in turn was monitored by sensors stowed on the car's anti-lock brake system (ABS), with the correct amount of torque distributed to the front or rear wheels depending on axle or wheel slip. The centre and rear differentials could also be locked manually for extreme conditions.

Power for the new Carrera 4, and the forthcoming two-wheel-drive Carrera 2 model, came from an evolution of the previous generation's

1989 Porsche Carrera 4

Engine
Power unit: six-cylinder, horizontally opposed, air-cooled
Capacity: 3600cc
Location: rear
Valves: two valves per cylinder
Construction: aluminium/steel
Bore x stroke: 100mm x 76.4mm
Compression ratio: 11.8:1
Fuel system: Bosch sequential fuel injection
Power: 250bhp @ 6100rpm
Torque: 228lb/ft @ 4800rpm
Transmission: five-speed manual or four-speed Tiptronic

Suspension
Front: independent MacPherson struts, lower wishbones, coil springs, Bilstein dampers, anti-roll bar
Rear: semi-trailing arms, coil springs, gas dampers, anti-roll bar

Brakes
Front and rear: ventilated discs, four-pot calipers

Wheels
Front: Alloy, 6J x 16in
Rear: Alloy, 8J x 16in

Tyres
Front: 205/55ZR16
Rear: 225/50ZR16

Dimensions
Length: 4250mm
Wheelbase: 2271mm
Width: 1651mm
Weight: 1450kg

Performance
Maximum speed: 162mph
0–60mph: 5.7 seconds

Above *The 3.6-litre engine of the 1990 911 Carrera 4 produced 250bhp and an enviable speed of 162mph.*

Right *What initially appears to be a ventilation grille actually houses the rising rear spoiler, a hallmark of the model.*

3.2-litre engine. There was just one criterion for the new engine, and the new car: that it should be more powerful and quicker than the outgoing 3.2 Carrera. To achieve this goal, the engine's capacity grew to 3.6 litres, new forged pistons were inserted, and the compression ratio was raised yet again to 11.8:1. The modified engine also had to be designed to run with or without catalytic converters, which were quickly becoming mandatory requirements in many of the 911's core markets. The fitting of a revised Bosch Motronic ignition and injection system ensured that the new cars produced the same 250bhp and 228lb/ft, or torque, no matter which market they were in. Porsche also claimed the Carrera 2 and 4 to have an identical set of performance figures, both cars capable of reaching a 162mph maximum speed and completing the 0–60mph sprint in 5.7 seconds.

With the radical changes in the engine came a development of the 3.2 Carrera's five-speed manual gearbox, which featured stronger ratios across the range in order to cope with the additional power and torque now being developed, and a taller fifth-gear ratio. The new Carrera 4 and 2 911s also saw the introduction of Porsche's four-speed semi-automatic Tiptronic gearbox, revolutionary by reason of its versatility: it could be driven as a regular automatic transmission, or should the driver wish to take a little more control, the selector lever could be slid across the gate, pushed forward for a higher gear and pulled back for a lower. While adding a new dimension to the experience of driving an automatic Porsche, even when 'semi-automatic' mode was selected the brain controlling the electronics within the gearbox would still have the final say as to whether the driver could change gear at will.

With four-wheel drive now fitted to the 911, the car's suspension needed to be redesigned. The presence of the front drive shafts and differential required the original torsion bars to be removed and the MacPherson strut to have its springs fitted over the strut. A slightly thinner anti-roll bar was also introduced, as was power steering, due to the increased weight of the four-wheel-drive system. The new model's rear suspension employed the previous-generation Turbo's aluminium semi-trailing arm set-up, with coil springs working independently of the existing shock absorbers. As with the front suspension, a smaller-diameter anti-roll bar was fitted to the rear – testament to the fact that the Porsche engineers felt they had moved the 911's game on considerably with this new model.

The new C4 and C2 also featured completely new brakes, although they had started life as a derivative that had first been fitted to the 928 S4. With their 298mm (front) and 299mm (rear) ventilated discs clamped by new four-piston calipers, and with cool air directed on to them from air ducts neatly crafted into the car's front bumper, 964 drivers would never find the car's braking performance wanting. A new alloy wheel design was also introduced, the front wheels measuring 6 x 16in and wearing 205/55ZR tyres and the rears 8 x 16in with 225/50ZR profile tyres.

With the 3.6-litre Carrera 4 and Carrera 2 Porsche had laid down the foundations on which to carry the 911 forward. As a company it had come through a boom period, and was surviving the global recession of the late 1980s with equal success. Sales were steadily increasing, the marque was regaining its credibility, and the world was ready for the next incarnation of the most famous sports car of them all.

Below The Carrera 2. This example, dating from 1993, has few visible differences from the 3.6-litre Carrera 4 and shared the same performance figures.

Above *All-wheel driving the 1990 911 Carrera 4 chassis.*

Top *A cutaway view of the 1990 911 Carrera 4.*

Opposite *A new generation: the 993. This is a 1995 911 Carrera. Note the smoother lines and more robust-looking appearance of this model.*

MODEL IN FOCUS: 964 CARRERA 4

The year 1988 was the twenty-fifth anniversary of the 911, and it just so happened to mark a significant milestone in the model's evolution: for the 1989 model year (first seen in 1988), Porsche introduced the first production-ready four-wheel-drive 911. With its new, sleeker lines, the Carrera 4 brought a fresh look to the 911 stable and took the marque into new territory.

The four-wheel-drive system had first been seen on the 959 supercar, but had been simplified for this run-of-the-mill production car (if such a term is appropriate to any Porsche). Where 911s that had gone before had proved tricky to handle at the limit, and appeared to revel in throwing their unwary pilots through a hedge (backwards, normally) at the earliest opportunity, the Carrera 4 provided more than an element of surefootedness that had never been seen before in a 911. No longer would lifting off the throttle mid-corner result in a nasty and expensive hedge/911 interface; rather, the car could be controlled, finessed, and more importantly enjoyed by mere mortals who didn't have the reactions of the era's Formula One heroes such as Ayrton Senna and Alain Prost.

Not that this went down too well with the hardest 911 fanatics. Porsches, and 911s in particular, shouldn't be easy to drive or simple to master. They were driving machines in the purest form of the phrase; should the driver be unable to control his steed, then perhaps he should look elsewhere. But Porsche was not in a position to appeal to a limited, narrow-minded market. In the C4 the 911 had to all intents and purposes been tamed, and it found favour again with those looking for a true sports car that was not only a joy to drive but possessed the reliability and mechanical security missing from the Italian, British and Japanese competition. The yuppies loved it, Porsche reaped the rewards and moved forward, all four wheels pulling in the right direction.

THE 993 GENERATION

From the moment the new 993 was launched in 1994, Porsche had trouble keeping up with demand. With the 993 Porsche had successfully reinvented a car that had, looking back, merely had a succession of face-lifts, albeit some of them thorough. The 993, though, was the first true new 911 since the original car had been launched way back in 1963 and was the result of Porsche's management insisting that the family's latest member must be improved in three distinct areas: looks, engine and handling.

Visually, the car had been brought bang up to date. The classic 911 profile was still there, yet somehow the designers had managed to produce a successor that looked totally different. It had taken on a more muscular stance, as if it had been injected with steroids and sent to the gym for a vigorous workout. Only the doors and front bonnet were carried over from the 964-generation car, which allowed the engineers to design and build an altogether stiffer body (by some 20 per cent) with no weight increase. Significant aerodynamic tweaks were made to the car's front and rear bumper assemblies, which not only improved airflow over and around the car but directed cooling more efficiently into vital areas such as the front brakes and the rear engine compartment. The new 911 also featured an evolution of the 964 model's electronically controlled rear spoiler. Operational at the same speeds (rising at 50mph, descending at 6mph), the spoiler sat flusher with the engine cover, again to improve airflow.

There were also key improvements to the 911's cabin. In the past the cabins of successive generations had been enhanced by nothing

1993 Porsche 911

Engine
Power unit: six cylinder, horizontally opposed, air-cooled
Capacity: 3600cc
Location: rear
Valves: two valves per cylinder
Construction: all aluminium
Bore x stroke: 100mm x 76.4mm
Compression ratio: 11.3:1
Fuel system: Bosch Motronic engine management
Power: 272bhp @ 6100rpm
Torque: 243lb/ft @ 5000rpm
Transmission: six-speed manual

Suspension
Front: independent MacPherson struts, lower wishbones, coil springs and dampers, anti-roll bar
Rear: multi-link, coil springs and dampers, anti-roll bar

Brakes
Front and rear: ventilated discs, four-piston calipers, ABS

Wheels
Front: 7J x 16in
Rear: 9J x 16in

Tyres
Front: 205/55ZR16
Rear: 245/45ZR16

Dimensions
Length: 4245mm
Wheelbase: 2271mm
Width: 1735mm
Weight: 1370kg

Performance
Maximum speed: 168mph
0–60mph: 5.6 seconds

more than the use of softer materials for dashboards and the like, and the fitting of additional switchgear; in the 993 model the seats were significantly revised to offer greater support all round and were electronically controllable and heated. A solution to the 911's biggest foible, heating, was also found with the incorporation of an electronically controlled heater unit. The days of waiting for your 911's air-cooled motor to warm up before you could were over. Other changes included driver and passenger airbags (another constraint forced upon the motor industry by government legislation), which required the 911 to be fitted with a rather unsporting four-spoke steering wheel.

Although remaining at 3.6-litre capacity, the 993 benefited from an additional 10 per cent more power than the 964 model, with peak power now some 272bhp at 6100rpm and maximum torque 243lb/ft at 5000rpm. Again, lighter pistons were fitted to the air-cooled unit and the crankshaft was strengthened, and metals such as magnesium were used for components such as the cooling fan and oil pump housing, although the new engine still weighed some 20kg more. An upgraded Bosch M2.10 engine management system was installed, complete with sequential multi-point fuel injection.

The biggest enhancement for the 911's flat-six engine, however, came in 1996 when Porsche introduced its VarioCam induction system to the standard car's air-cooled engine. Larger inlet and exhaust valves were also fitted, and these changes saw power climb to 282bhp at 6100rpm and 251lb/ft torque at 5250rpm. First seen on the 1995 Carrera RS, VarioCam was a Porsche-patented design which altered the length of the inlet pipe according to the engine revs, thus improving the volumetric efficiency at different

Opposite page
Top A cutaway view of the 993-generation Carrera 2.
Bottom The engine compartment of the 911 Carrera (1993 model).

This page The 1993 911 Carrera. Note the revised cabin layout, including the four-spoke steering wheel required to house the statutory driver's airbag.

Above *The last of the air-cooled 911s: the*
sleek and perfectly-proportioned 993 Carrera.

engine speeds. Not only did this improve the car's performance, it also helped to reduce exhaust emissions and enhance fuel economy.

In terms of transmission the 993 was offered with a six-speed manual or four-speed Tiptronic gearbox (which in 1995 was the Tiptronic S) which enabled the driver to change gear semi-automatically via either the conventional gear selector on the floor or two buttons on the steering wheel. Initially the 993 carried over the same four-wheel-drive sunning gear as the 964 model, but in 1995 this was heavily re-engineered to be both lighter, smoother and faster, responding to each wheel's level of grip. This provided the benefit of extra control at the limit in treacherous conditions, and should the driver lift off the throttle abruptly in a corner, the four-wheel-drive's ability to brake a spinning wheel effectively cured the 911's inherent handling problems as a result of having its engine placed beyond the rear axle line.

In the 993 Porsche took the decision to scrap the 911's traditional semi-trailing arm rear suspension and replace it with a multi-link arrangement. The new rear axle looked similar to the dual-wishbone axle fitted to a race car, with the same cast-aluminium two-piece subframes. The coil springs were fitted over the gas-filled shock absorbers to provide the much-improved, smoother ride Porsche had set out to achieve with the 993. The car's front suspension remained pretty much unchanged, although every component was redesigned to save over three kilograms in weight, again to improve the car's ride, lighten its steering action and reduce vibrations. Sports suspension was available as an option, which featured shorter, stiffer springs and anti-roll bars together with stiffer dampers.

Though the 993's discs remained the same diameter as the 964's, they were now ventilated and cross-drilled, clamped by larger four-pot calipers and controlled by Porsche's latest ABS 5 system. Larger 7 x 16in (front) and 9 x 16in (rear) low-pressure cast alloy wheels were designed and fitted to suck hot air away from the brakes, and they wore 205/55ZR tyres on the front and 245/45ZRs at the rear.

No matter which model 993 you drove, it was immediately apparent that the 911 had come of age. Its radically new design had become not only the most recognizable but one of the most attractive of the time. And on top of all this the 911 was fitted with unbreakable mechanicals and was built to last as long as its lucky owner wanted it to.

That the 993 also spawned some of the greatest 911 derivatives of all time – so many, in fact, that this book dedicates a whole chapter to them and other special 911s (chapter 7) – is testament to just how accomplished the car had become.

The fact that Porsche arrived at this beautifully honed vehicle when it did is fitting, because as the sun set on 1997 the air-cooled 911 had come to the end of its long and illustrious life. Still, you can drive every new Porsche since 1997, whether a Boxster, a 911 or the forthcoming Cayenne, as much as you like but there's nothing that comes close to feeling and hearing the intoxicating howl produced by that air-cooled flat-six sitting behind you.

GOING TOPLESS: THE PORSCHE 911 CABRIOLET AND TARGA

An open-top car has been included within the Porsche model line-up since 1948, and it was only two years into the 911's production life before open-air motoring became available to the 911 driver. Rather than produce a traditional, fully retractable roofed car, Porsche produced the Targa (named after its successes in the Targa Florio road races) and designed it to comply with what Porsche engineers believed – incorrectly, as it turned out – to be impending US safety legislation stipulating that a roll-over bar must be fitted to protect the occupants of a convertible in the event of an accident. There was another issue to address, one that had come to light through experience with the previous 356 convertible, which became progressively tiring to drive at speed with the hood up due to buffeting and wind noise.

Below *A splendid example of the Porsche 911T Targa 2.4. Produced to popular acclaim in 1965, the design evolved through the 1970s and continues to be a favoured model today. This is a 1973 model.*

Unveiled at the 1965 Frankfurt Motor Show, the new Targa went into production the very next year and was available with either a removable plastic section or a collapsible hood, both of which could be stowed in the front luggage compartment. The plastic rear window was held in place with a zip under the roll-bar, though not only did it add to the noise problem they had tried to eliminate, it also leaked! A solution was found for the 1969 model year, when the definitive Targa top was standardized as the removable plastic panel and the zip-in rear window was replaced with a fixed piece of moulded glass. Although with this configuration the car was less of a convertible, at least it had been made more snug and watertight.

Although the demand for a convertible 911 had been partially met by the arrival of the Targa, in the late 1970s Porsche's marketing arm aired its desire for a full-fledged convertible 911 model. However, the then boss Dr Ernst Fuhrmann was adamant that the front-engined 928 coupé would replace the 911 and he saw no reason to sanction a new and costly convertible derivative of the rear-engined sports car. As a result of that decision, along with a number of others that in the eyes of Ferry Porsche devalued the 911 – and it was his baby, after all – Fuhrmann was 'retired' from the company. His replacement, Peter Schutz, put in place at the beginning of 1981, just happened to have similar views to Porsche as to how the 911 should evolve.

The Frankfurt Show was yet again the venue for the new 911 derivative, which appeared alongside the 3-litre Carrera, and this time it was a full convertible model featuring a four-wheel-drive platform that would eventually

appear on the 959 supercar some six years later. Initial fears that the removal of the Targa's roll-over bar would seriously harm the car's rigidity were unfounded: the new convertible was as stiff as the regular car, although some minor reinforcement was required to the car's structural areas.

The Cabriolet's hood could be raised and lowered in a single movement, and to keep buffeting to a minimum the hood was braced with longitudinal aluminium reinforcement. The rear window, which was zipped into place, could also be removed when the hood was in its raised position.

The car was originally offered with the 3.2-litre Carrera models for the 1984 season, and in 1987 was not only available with turbocharged power, but spawned the Speedster derivative. Initially put forward as the 911 Cabriolet's first design in 1981 by Schutz, the Speedster had to wait in the wings until the 1987 Frankfurt Motor Show to get its first public viewing, before going on sale in 1989. Using the Cabriolet's body shell, but with additional body stiffening, the new model was distinguishable from its convertible cousin by its aluminium-framed windscreen raked down by a further five degrees over the regular Cabriolet.

There was also a new simplified hood, termed by the factory an 'emergency' or 'temporary' hood to reinforce the message that it was not built to the same high standards of comfort offered by the Cabriolet's hood. Owners were also warned that the hood might not be waterproof, and should not be put through a car wash. In addition, customers were asked to sign a disclaimer saying that they would accept 'a degree of wind noise and water ingress from the seal areas in inclement weather'. The hood was stowed under a colour-coded polyurethane moulding designed to improve aerodynamics, though that forced the rear shape of the car to take on an awkward bulkiness. There were no real thrills to the Speedster, with its manual windows and heater, though the factory did claim a 70kg weight saving over the coupé. It was the last 911 model to be built in the old Zuffenhausen factory on a body shell based on the original 1963 design.

This page The 1989 Speedster. Here you can clearly see the bulky area behind the seats that was used to stow the soft-top and the distinctive flared rear arches reminiscent of the first 911s.

Opposite page The 1984 911 Carrera Cabriolet. Featuring four-wheel drive (only later models offered turbo power) and a 3-litre engine.

Below *An attractive new Carrera for the Nineties, the 1994 Cabriolet came with a dazzling array of drive and transmission options as well as the usual luxury extras.*

Opposite page *The new Targa had bags of style, a fully electrically retractable roof and even sun blinds! Note how the central rollbar has been replaced by side supports on this 1996 model.*

The Speedster reappeared in 1992 on the 964 platform, and was marketed much more aggressively as a sports convertible, with its Recaro bucket seats, seventeen-inch Cup design alloy wheels, and a number of options to produce the illusion that it was something special. Whether or not that was the case, of course, was and is open to debate. To many, though, the Speedster's sleeker lines (helped by the less bulky hood cover), lower windscreen and general stance certainly made it stand out from the regular Cabriolets and Targas.

With the introduction of the 993 model 911, Porsche not only introduced an attractive, practical and secure Cabriolet which was available in either two- or four-wheel drive, six-speed manual or four-speed Tiptronic, they moved the Targa goalposts. Based on the regular 993 Cabriolet model, the new Targa was just 30kg heavier than the regular 911 coupé and was available with the same 285bhp VarioCam 3.6-litre engine as the rest of the 911 range, and as a manual or Tiptronic. The Targa also sported its own unique design of seventeen-inch alloy wheel. More importantly, though, the new model had a glass roof. Yes, the new 993 generation 911 Targa featured a fully retractable glass roof panel which at the touch of a button would slide from the leading edge of the windscreen down and beneath the rear window to provide open-air motoring with the security of a coupé. With a small but effective glass deflector popping up at the front of the roof, the noise and buffeting was no worse – in fact, some said noticeably better – than driving a coupé model with the sunroof open. Thermally insulated, and containing a special ultraviolet filter to give protection to the car's occupants from the glare and heat of the sun, it also featured an electrically operated roller-blind to keep interior temperatures at a comfortable level. The enlarged glass area also furnished the 911's cabin with more space. This new Targa design was possible because rather than install a roll-over bar, as in the original Targas, the new model featured two longitudinal rails that ran from the top of the windscreen to the base of the rear window, providing the necessary support required for a roll-over incident.

chapter
five

The
Unsung
Heroes

Think of a Porsche and you'll instinctively think 911. Put the legendary sports coupé aside and think again, and you'll probably come up with the Boxster or the new-for-2002 Cayenne off-roader. Think beyond those and you'll probably start talking about the quartet of front-engined, water-cooled coupés, the 968, 928, 944, and 924. And then there's always the original Porsche, the 356. You might be thinking super Porsche, and then we are talking the 959. But there's more to Porsche than these distinctive cars. Two other models have played just as important a role in the development, expansion and success of the most profitable car company in the world, cars that have saved the firm from failure and allowed the Stuttgart engineers a platform on which to experiment. They are the unsung heroes of the Porsche oeuvre, lacking the recognition they unarguably deserve, not to mention the devoted following some of their less deserving cousins went on to enjoy. For in the rear-engined 912 and mid-engined 914, Porsche had two highly competent but underrated driving machines.

THE 912

Porsche had always planned for the 911 line-up to feature a less powerful, four-cylinder air-cooled engine; even four of the thirteen 911 prototypes were thus equipped. The thinking behind this was simple. Even though the 911 was first conceived as a replacement for the original 356, the new car was always going to cost a whole lot more than Porsche's first production car. Not wishing to lose any of the loyal customers who had supported his fledgling company during its early years, Ferry Porsche was conscious of the need to offer his new car at a price affordable to existing customers while at the same time broadening the appeal of the Porsche brand.

The four-cylinder 912 was introduced in 1965, two years after the 911 went into production, and it immediately provided the quickly developing Porsche enthusiast with something to get excited about. Visually the new car was indistinguishable from its six-cylinder bigger brother, which meant that it used the same platform and independent suspension layout, comprising MacPherson struts for the front and the semi-trailing arm set-up for the rear. Ultimately,

Previous page The neatly-packaged 914/6, a typical mid-Seventies model from the Zuffenhausen factory.

Right and opposite page The affordable Porsche: a 1965 912. From a distance it is easily mistakable for the 911, but the first models inherited body parts from the 356 as well as a new four-cylinder engine. The 912 was also known as the 'Europe Type' because it was never made available elsewhere in the world, despite its early popularity.

however, the 912's ride was a good deal smoother and less focused than that of the 911. The new car also featured the 911's gearbox, although initially it was only offered with four gears (a five-speed gearbox was available soon after the model's introduction, however). Other 911 carry-overs included the aluminium body (obviously) and, as a demonstration of how highly Porsche rated the 912 in the line of its model development, when the 911's wheelbase grew an additional 57mm in 1969, so did the 912's. Porsche also took this opportunity to furnish the 912 with identical body parts to the 911, including such items as wing mirrors, headlamp surrounds and air vents, which had previously been donated by the 356.

The 356 in fact donated much more than just the odd bit of chrome to the 912. The 912's interior featured seats and a heating and ventilation system first seen in the 356, while the new

Top *The interior of the Porsche 912, which reused a number of 356 components.*

Above *The bizarre and futuristic Tapiro 912 concept car of 1970, designed by Italdesign with input from Porsche and VW. It featured twin sets of gullwing doors, one for the passenger cabin and one for stowage.*

Opposite page *The Gugelot-designed Porsche 914, developed with VW, featured a mid-mounted engine, Porsche's first. It didn't capture the public imagination though, partly because it just didn't look like a Porsche.*

car rode on the 4.5 x 15in steel wheels from the same model. The 356's disc brakes were also carried over, as, of course, was that car's four-cylinder engine. Although detuned to 90bhp, produced at 5800rpm, and with just 86lb/ft of torque on offer at 3500rpm (in the 356, the engine was tuned to produce 95bhp and 90lb/ft of torque), the 912 was capable of reaching 60mph from a standstill in 11.6 seconds and going on to a 115mph maximum. The 356C took thirteen seconds but could go one mile an hour quicker thanks to its super-smooth shape. By using the 356's engine, Porsche not only benefited financially, but went some way towards curing the 911's inherent oversteer problem. With the four-cylinder engine weighing considerably less than that of the 911's new flat-six unit, the 912's overall weight was reduced by 130kg to 935kg, which provided the car with a much sweeter handling balance. When the lengthened chassis was introduced, the handling gulf between the cars was increased yet further.

This combination of 911 good looks, cheaper purchase price, lower running costs and friendlier handling characteristics saw the model rack up more than 30,000 sales during its first four years of production. But its time in the Porsche show rooms was soon over. The 911 had started to find favour, its reputation as a pure driver's car (i.e. a bit of a handful) affording its owners the opportunity to say, 'Look, everybody, I can tame the 911!' before pirouetting off into the countryside. 911 sales matched and then comprehensively overtook those of the 912, and with an all-new 'entry-level' Porsche ('poor man's Porsche' never sounds right) ready and waiting in the wings, 912 production finally ceased in 1969 – though not before a 912 Targa had had the honour of being the 100,000th Porsche to be made, and not before a 912 rally car had won the 1967 European Rally Championship.

Or rather, the 912 went into hibernation for six years, for it reappeared in 1975 with the same classic looks as the 911 of the time and with a larger-capacity, more powerful 2-litre engine. The 912's replacement model, the mid-engined 914 documented later in this chapter, had lasted just six years in production before it was deemed to have run its course and found itself set to be replaced by yet another all-new model, the front-engined, water-cooled 924.

But we digress. With the all-new 924 not quite production-ready, Porsche reintroduced the 912, a move which to the cynical world outside was nothing more than a stop-gap measure verging on the desperate. Which of course it was. The 911 had evolved into a fine sports car. Its model line had grown to provide desirable and extremely accomplished driving machines sought after by enthusiasts and successful people the world over. It had elevated Porsche to a level never previously seen in the automotive industry and left a yawning gap in Porsche's model line-up. Where the 911 was the model to aspire to, the 914 had been the début car to start customers off on the Porsche ladder. With that now discontinued, entry to the world of Porsche meant parting with an expensive joining fee.

So the 912 was reintroduced, now tagged the 912E with, on paper, a tantalizing specification. It was dressed in the current 911's svelte and stylish body, which was mated to the same car's longer wheelbase, and featured identical front and rear suspension to the more powerful 911. Engine capacity had expanded, with the fitting of the Volkswagen-sourced 2-litre four-cylinder engine that had previously been coupled to the superseded 914. However, even though it had the same power output as the previous generation's 912 some six years earlier, a further 12lb/ft of torque (up to 98lb/ft) and fuel injection – hence the 'E' prefix, which stands for 'Einspritzung', the German for fuel injection – the new car was both slower to 60mph (thirteen seconds) and lagged by 5mph when it came to maximum speed, not helped by the 197kg excess in weight carried by the 912E over the original car.

Despite its practicality during the fuel crisis era, the reintroduced model was too heavy and too slow to capture the first-time Porsche buyer's imagination. Parked, it might have had the appearance of a 911, there the likeness ended. In hindsight, the 912E did the firm more damage than good, and the model sold fewer than two thousand units during its one-year production run. Had it not been for its lacklustre performance in the showroom and on the road, the previous-generation 912 might not have been labelled with the 'poor man's Porsche' tag.

Even today the 912 suffers from a bit of an identity crisis, with prices for good, clean, original examples starting at a similar level to the equivalent aged and conditioned 911. Where the 912 was once seen as a worthy alternative to the then expensive 911, today it competes head-on with the 911, and unfortunately for the 912 it just doesn't have the muscle.

THE 914

In the 912 Porsche had developed a model that appealed to the masses because of its close links with the marque-leading 911 coupé. Here was a car that to all intents and purposes was a 911. It had its engine in the right place, it looked identical, and in terms of performance, in the right

1965 Porsche 912

Engine
Power unit: four-cylinder, horizontally opposed, air-cooled
Capacity: 1582cc
Location: rear
Valves: two valves per cylinder
Construction: aluminium
Bore x stroke: 82.5mm x 74mm
Compression ratio: 8.5:1
Fuel system: carburettors
Power: 90bhp @ 5800rpm
Torque: 86lb/ft @ 3500rpm
Transmission: four-speed manual, rear-wheel drive

Suspension
Front: independent MacPherson struts, lower wishbones, torsion bar springs, anti-roll bar
Rear: independent trailing arms, transverse torsion bar springs, telescopic dampers, anti-roll bar

Brakes
Front and rear: un-servoed discs

Wheels
Front and rear: steel, 4.5J x 15in

Tyres
Front and rear: 165 x 15in

Dimensions
Length: 4163mm
Wheelbase: 2268mm
Width: 1610mm
Weight: 935kg

Performance
Maximum speed: 115mph
0–60mph: 11.6 seconds

1970 Porsche 914 1.7

Engine

Power unit: four-cylinder, horizontally opposed, air-cooled
Capacity: 1679cc
Location: mid-engined
Valves: two valves per cylinder
Construction: aluminium
Bore x stroke: 90mm x 66mm
Compression ratio: 8.2:1
Fuel system: Bosch D-Jetronic injection
Power: 80bhp
Torque: 100lb/ft
Transmission: five-speed manual

Suspension

Front: independent MacPherson struts, lower wishbones, torsion bar springs, anti-roll bar
Rear: independent trailing arms, transverse torsion bar springs, telescopic dampers, anti-roll bar

Brakes

Front and rear: un-servoed discs

Wheels

Front and rear: steel, 5.5J x 14in

Tyres

Front: 175/70R14
Rear: 180/80R14

Dimensions

Length: 4050mm
Wheelbase: 2450mm
Width: 1650mm
Weight: 970kg

Performance

Maximum speed: 110mph
0–60mph: 12.4 seconds

Above *This rear view of the Porsche 914 shows off its distinctive targa top and large boot, which offered considerable stowage space.*

conditions it wouldn't be a million miles behind when snaking around on a piece of tarmac. Just as today BMW 318i owners are keen to fit the factory's M Sport body kit to create the illusion that their lowly four-cylinder coupé is on a par with the cooking M3, a 912 passed the all-important drive-by test. It looked the part. It looked like a Porsche.

And perhaps therein lay the problem for the all-new, mid-engined Porsche 914. The 911 had become Porsche; anything else with a different model name was an impostor, a fake, not the real deal. That the 914 was co-developed with Volkswagen only fuelled its subsequent rejection.

The model grew out of this collaboration between Porsche and Volkswagen and was based on the realization by the former that it needed what is termed today 'an entry-level' machine, working in conjunction with the latter's natural desire to broaden its appeal with a model that was altogether more appealing than its 'people car', the Beetle. There were, of course, already links between these two companies. The original 356 prototype coupés were based on VW's Beetle platform, a car that had been designed by Ferdinand Porsche, but it wasn't until VW's chairman Heinrich Nordhoff agreed to a meeting with Ferry Porsche in the mid-1960s that the idea for the joint venture was conceived. While VW had its own agenda for committing to the project, Porsche had one simple motive: the 911 had become too expensive and they could no longer rely on the 912 to attract new customers to the brand. Porsche also craved to build a mid-engined production car in a similar mould to the 904 racer, so this proposed new model could kill the proverbial two birds with one stone.

A deal was eventually struck between the two manufacturers which provided for the production of a two-seater, mid-engined roadster to be powered by either a new VW-designed and -built Bosch fuel-injected flat-four air-cooled engine or the much acclaimed Porsche flat-six complete with Weber carburettors. The two firms also agreed that coachbuilder Karmann should construct the body. The 914 design was penned by another German company, Gugelot Design, who had been approached some years earlier by Porsche, having expressed an interest in becoming involved in future sports car projects. The only condition placed on the design of the new car was that it must not resemble any previous Porsche or Volkswagen models, and although Gugelot's initial drawings for a new (Porsche) sports car were based on a front-engined design, these were easily rectified in order to meet the mid-engine layout stipulations.

A great number of designs were submitted to Karmann, varying in shape from futuristic wedge styles to more traditional looks. The eventual crisp, squared-off design met all the criteria. It featured a removable Targa roof panel, provided ample luggage space for weekends away, and looked nothing like any Porsche or VW that had gone before it.

Work started on the first prototypes in 1967, and when the first four-cylinder car was unveiled on 1 March 1968 it earned the immediate approval of both parties. The project continued apace until in the following month, April, the two companies suffered a damaging blow with the death of Heinrich Nordhoff, who had handed the VW reins over to Kurt Lotz the previous year. The project was put on hold while Lotz insisted on a more formal contract

Above *Cutaway view of the Porsche 914/6, showing its mid-mounted air-cooled flat-six engine.*

between VW, Porsche and Karmann. Up to that point, as it transpired, they had been working on nothing more secure than a verbal agreement.

The new car had already been christened the 914 by Porsche by the time production started in not one but two different factories. The four-cylinder-engined cars would be completely assembled by Karmann in Osnabrück, from where as unpainted body shells they would be transferred to Zuffenhausen for assembly with Porsche's six-cylinder unit, alongside the Porsche 911. Eventually this process became too impractical, and a brand-new facility was constructed in Ludwigsburg, close to Porsche's Zuffenhausen factory. The company set up to market the new car was VW-Porsche Vertriebgesellschaft GmbH, and Klaus Schneider took charge of selling the 914 in all markets except North America, where Volkswagen of America would handle sales under its newly created Porsche+Audi Division. The cars would still, however, be badged as Porsches and sold through Porsche dealerships. Throughout the rest of the world the 914 would be badged with the confusing VW–Porsche nomenclature, a decision that would plague the model throughout its short life.

The first 914 was launched to the public in 1969 and featured a 1.7-litre 80bhp four-cylinder air-cooled engine. Even though the new Porsche weighed in at a modest 970kg, the original 914's outright performance didn't make it into the category marked 'electrifying'; lukewarm was closer to the mark. The 0–60mph dash was completed in 12.4 seconds and the maximum speed was just 110mph. Understandably, perhaps, magazine road tests at the time concentrated on the new car's dynamics, which if nothing else enabled Porsche to show that it could make rewarding, fun and safe cars for all to drive at the limit. MacPherson struts with coil springs and oil-filled dampers suspended the front of the 914, while the rear featured a

Above *The 914/6 featured a six-cylinder engine and several minor improvements over the 914, including an interior update.*

semi-trailing arm set-up with torsion bars and coil springs. Add all that to the car's mid-engined layout, which afforded it near-perfect weight distribution, and the 914 was a beautifully balanced car, settling quickly into corners and providing the driver with uninterrupted feedback through the steering.

The issue about outright performance was soon answered with the arrival of the flat-six-engined 914/6. Taken straight from the 911T, this 2-litre air-cooled unit produced 110bhp at 5800rpm (though it is believed this figure was actually closer to 120bhp) and 116lb/ft of torque at 4200rpm. Performance was just as strong: the 0–60mph dash was completed in a mere 8.8 seconds, and the maximum speed recorded was a healthy 123mph.

The six-cylinder also featured uprated brakes over its four-cylinder sibling. Off came the solid VW-sourced front brake discs and on went a pair of ventilated items kindly donated by the 911. The four-cylinder car's VW steering column was also replaced by a 911 version on the six-cylinder car. Porsche also applied a thick under-body sealant to the Karmann-produced shells in an attempt to prevent rust, though they proved just as susceptible to it as the untreated four-cylinder cars. Other differences between the two included shorter ratios for the 914/6, different style wheels and detailed badging and interior trim variations. It was, of course, the 911-engined car's performance that set it apart, and this is what would ultimately trip the 914 up.

The basic problem lay in cost. Existing Volkswagen owners found the Porsche connection too exotic for their tastes, and for the Porsche enthusiasts, whether an existing owner or an aspiring one, it was too expensive for what was supposed to be an entry-level model. In 1970, the year the cars went on sale in the UK, a 1.7-litre 914 cost £2,165, while the 914/6 was just £200 cheaper than the more powerful, and to many eyes prettier, 2.2-litre 911T at £3,475. Put simply, the basic car was too expensive for the performance it offered, and the headlining model was too expensive for the same reason.

Although it is thought to have cost Porsche and VW somewhere in the region of £70 million in today's money, the decision was taken to keep the project afloat. The 1973 model year saw the introduction of a new 2-litre four-cylinder air-cooled engine. A development of the original 1.7-litre unit, the new engine produced a respectable 100bhp and 105lb/ft of torque, and afforded the new model a 116mph maximum speed. Had the 914's prayers been answered? Yes and no. The entry-level 914 was now able to perform to a degree expected of a car of this cost; unfortunately, these performance gains also made the 914/6 even more of a white elephant. Production would stop by the year's end for the 911-engined roadster, and the original 1.7-litre engine was dropped the following year (yes – rather bewilderingly, Porsche had offered both the 1.7-litre and 2-litre cars to an unwilling public).

In place of this entry-level 914 came a 1.8-litre derivative that could be equipped with a Bosch L-Jetronic fuel injection system for the US market or dual twin-choke Weber carburettors for Europe. European customers were the beneficiaries of this change. With ever-tightening emissions legislation in the US, the fuel-injected cars produced just 76bhp, 4bhp down on the outgoing, smaller-capacity engine. With the Weber carburettors fitted, power climbed to 85bhp. It was these two engines that would live in the 914 until its total departure from the Porsche line-up in 1976.

The 1973 model year saw the 914 come in for a number of other technical revisions, in particular the adoption of a 911-style side-shift gear linkage. Originally, the 914 was fitted with a tail-shift gear selector, which meant the linkage was fitted to the back of the gearbox, which was at the very rear of the engine. To say that an early 914's gear change is less than smooth or easy to shift cleanly and quickly is a wild understatement of the facts. Unfortunately, the car's brakes were always overlooked when it came to development, and as the power and performance climbed the inadequacies of the VW- and Porsche-sourced brakes began to show.

However, there was no denying that the 914 had become a quietly competent machine, which is why, even though it had found it hard to win favour with diehard Stuttgart fans (911 owners, mostly), when the 914 was dropped at the tail end of 1976 it wasn't down to Porsche's reluctance with the project, it was more to do with a change of heart by VW's new chief Rudolf Leiding, who had taken over from Lotz and was preparing to launch VW into a new era. While 914 fans took great delight in the ill-fated VW air-cooled K70 saloon, they retreated quietly with the introduction of a new front-wheel-drive hatchback.

It would be nice to think the 914 had offered something to the VW Golf, but while the Wolfsburg firm sprinted ahead in its transformation into one of the world's biggest car manufacturers, Porsche found itself caught on the brink of its darkest hour. Ironically, it was the introduction of Porsche's current six-cylinder, mid-engined roadster that saved the company from failure during the recession-recovering 1990s, and following initial scepticism from the Porsche hardcore the Boxster is a fully paid-up member of the exclusive club that is Porsche.

Above Problems with rust and reliability weren't the only thing affecting the 914/6's sales. Badged as a VW-Porsche everywhere other than the USA, it was too costly for VW's market and Porsche's customers viewed it with suspicion.

chapter
six

The
Front-engined
Coupés

Think Porsche, think rear-engined? Think air-cooling and boxer configuration? Think again. Four-cylinder, front-engined, water-cooled cars account for over 30 per cent of all Porsches ever produced. For almost two decades from 1975 they were an integral part of the range, in 924, 928, 944 and 968 form. At times it was believed that one or another of these models could supplant the 911 as the Porsche staple, yet they all passed away in the mid-1990s, unloved by many and mourned by few.

Though the 924 appeared first (in 1975), it was actually the big, expensive, V8-engined 928 that was first conceived as a saviour for the company. In 1972, when Ferry Porsche handed over the reins to Dr Ernst Fuhrmann (already famous in Porsche circles as the inventor of the fabled quad-cam Carrera flat-four engine), decades of family control, family design, family in-fighting and the towering influence of Ferdinand Porsche came to an end. And the company headed off in a new direction.

THE 924

The VW-Porsche Vertriebgesellschaft, which had been formed to market the 914, had foreseen that the 914 would not have the long-lived appeal that the classic 356 had enjoyed. However, sales of almost 120,000 cars during a six-year production run were too tempting to overlook, so a plan was hatched for Porsche to design a new model, which was to be marketed as either a VW or an Audi.

Like the 356, this was a Porsche that used VW suspension, steering, brakes and powerplants. It was to have a similar interior space to the 911, improved comfort, a usable boot space, and it must utilize as many VW parts as possible. It was also to be similar to the 928 (which we look at later in this chapter) in both looks and technical specification, and needed to offer 2+2 accommodation.

The chosen engine was a water-cooled four-cylinder unit already used in the VW range to power the LT van. For the new project it would be fuel-injected and mounted at the front. It was

Previous page *The first of the Grand Tourers, the water-cooled, front-engined 928.*

a fairly crude cast-iron affair, though, and drew criticism for its lack of refinement at higher engine speeds; furthermore, early models suffered from fuel vaporization and hot-start problems. Still, it gave 125bhp at 5800rpm and endowed the car with a top speed of 125mph and a 0–60mph time of just under ten seconds. To ensure close to 50–50 weight distribution the transmission was mounted at the rear, in a unit with the differential. Management liked this 'transaxle' set-up because it suited the Porsche tradition of technically challenging design. The upshot of this arrangement was that the new model was endowed with excellent balance and on-limit handling control. Suspension at the front was a hybrid of VW Beetle MacPherson struts and Golf lower arms, while the rear's semi-trailing arm and torsion bar set-up also came from the Beetle parts bin, as did the brakes. The four-speed Audi transmission did without the Porsche synchromesh system on the grounds of cost, while the steering rack came from the VW Golf, albeit with a higher ratio.

The dash design was reminiscent of the 911, but all the instruments, again, were from VW, and the new car gained a centre console soon after the first production models were launched. VW's cost-cutting demands had led to an interior that was both noisy and poorly built, although it soon evolved to become more adventurously Porsche in style. The exterior styling was the work of the young Harm Lagaay and was designed to reflect not only the 928, but also the curves and lines of Porsche's past. The clean contours and retractable headlamps, allied to the steeply raked screen, gave the car an impressively low drag coefficient of 0.34cd. It certainly scored well in terms of practicality. The small rear seats could accommodate children or fold forward to offer impressive load space through the glass hatchback.

The project became almost entirely VW when the joint-marketing organization was disbanded, but the oil crisis of 1973–4 had changed the motoring landscape and soon the car no longer featured in VW's future plans. Porsche, however, were convinced of its potential to succeed, and its dealers were desperate for a volume-selling model. It bought out the project for over $40 million at the beginning of 1975, contracting VW to build the car under Porsche

1976 Porsche 924

Engine
Power unit: four-cylinder, in-line, eight-valve head
Capacity: 2984cc
Location: front
Valves: two valves per cylinder
Construction: cast iron
Bore x stroke: 86.5mm x 84.4mm
Compression ratio: 9.3:1
Fuel system: Bosch K-Jetronic
Power: 125bhp @ 5800rpm
Torque: 122lb/ft @ 3000rpm
Transmission: five-speed manual, rear-wheel drive

Suspension
Front: independent MacPherson struts with coil springs, lower A-arms
Rear: independent semi-trailing arms, transverse torsion bars, tubular shocks

Brakes
Front: ventilated discs
Rear: drum

Wheels
Front and rear: 5.5 x 14in

Tyres
Front and rear: unknown

Dimensions
Length: 4213mm
Wheelbase: 2400mm
Width: 1676mm
Weight: 1065kg

Performance
Maximum speed: 125mph
0–60mph: 9.9 seconds

Opposite page: top *The rear view of an early 924 from 1975, showing its distinctive raked glass hatchback. Few were sold in this first year of manufacture but the market picked up in 1977, when a new automatic version was launched alongside the new 928.*

Opposite page: bottom *A 1977 example of the 924. Note the drop-down headlamps, previously used only on the 914 line, and the moulded-in light bar beneath, designed to hide the bumpers.*

Left *Cutaway view of the 924, with its water-cooled and front-mounted engine.*

Top *The last of the 924s, the S was an attempt to improve sales. It had little impact on the market despite adopting the Turbo's engine, and was retired after less than three years. This example dates from 1987.*

Above *Two special-edition 924s were produced, first a Martini-liveried version in 1986 and later this Le Mans version. A variant of the 924S, it was available only in 1988.*

quality control at the old VSU plant in Neckarsulm. The Porsche 924 was launched in November of that year.

Sales were slow for the first year, mainly due to the emission-strangled 95bhp US version, which lacked performance and therefore struggled to impress. But when a 110bhp version with three-speed automatic transmission appeared in 1977, sales took off. Almost 25,000 examples found a happy home that year. An intensely focused evolution would take place over the 924's lifespan in an attempt to distance it from its VW roots, and the 924 remained a smash hit in sales terms: the 100,000th example rolled off the production line in 1981, and 120,000 had been built by the time production ended in 1985.

Porsche had already launched a special-edition Martini-liveried 924 to celebrate its success in the 1976 World Championship of Makes, with the hope that this would push the 924's performance credentials, but it wasn't until production of the Turbo started in 1978 that the 924 could be considered a quick car. Visually, the Turbo was quite different from the stock 924, with four air intakes on the front bumper and a NACA duct on the bonnet designed to deliver a constant flow of cooling air over the turbocharger on the move. Underbody aerodynamics also aided engine cooling, while a black polyurethane rear spoiler aided stability and reduced drag. Wild and wacky interior trims were also introduced to lend a little pizazz to the range.

The real fizz, though, came from the engine. With a new alloy head and a number of uprated internals, it differed significantly from the stock VW unit. The star of the show was the KKK blower, which ran at 0.7bar and helped hoist power to 170bhp and torque over 180lb/ft. This shaved a full two seconds off the benchmark 0–60mph sprint and helped stretch flat-out speed to 140mph. The Turbo gained a further 7bhp in 1982 when an improved electronic management suite was fitted.

Perhaps the most significant 924 Turbos were the homologation specials, the Carrera GT and Carrera GTS. Designed for competition only, just 400 GTs were built. The wide arches gave the car extra visual impact, and they evolved into the shape of the 944. The GTS, with 245bhp and a top speed of 155mph, was madder still. It had a limited-slip differential, drilled brake discs, race-bred suspension and Fuchs alloy wheels, and the interior was stripped to shave 60kg off

This page The ultimate 924: the wild looks of the 1980 Carrera GT.

the Carrera GT's weight. It really was a road-going race car, but fewer than sixty were built, so very few got to experience its potent virtues.

The last of the 924s was the S. It was first introduced for the 1986 model year and lasted until June 1988. Audi no longer used cast-iron engines, and the relatively small numbers Porsche demanded didn't warrant their continued production. Owing mostly to continued criticism of the 2-litre engine's harshness and ever more stringent emissions standards, Porsche decided to use a 150bhp version of the 944's 2.5 litre mill. It gave the 924S respectable power – enough to warrant use of the Carrera GT's brakes anyway – and demand for the sleeker, more delicate lines was still there. For 1988, the S got exactly the same engine specification as the 944, giving 160bhp.

A Le Mans special edition, to commemorate win number twelve by Porsche, was the very last of the 924s. It was by this stage a far better car than the original – quicker, more refined and better-built – but the 924 never truly recovered from its dubious heritage and by the time of its demise it had been totally eclipsed by the 944.

MODEL IN FOCUS: 924 CARRERA GT

When the first design study of the Carrera GT broke cover at the 1979 Frankfurt Motor Show, the accompanying press release hailed the new car as a 'worthy successor to the 911 Carrera RS'. Porsche purists may find plenty to argue with in that statement, but in reality Porsche were planning to pull the plug on the 911 (imagine that!) in the not-too-distant future and it was hoped that the 924 Carrera GT would ease what would be a painful passing.

The Carrera GT was certainly the ultimate evolution of the 924, a true

Porsche 924 Carrera GT

Engine
Power unit: four-cylinder, single turbocharger with intercooler, water-cooled
Capacity: 1984cc
Location: front
Valves: two valves per cylinder
Construction: aluminium alloy
Bore x stroke: 86.5mm x 84.4mm
Compression ratio: 8.5:1
Fuel system: Bosch K-Jetronic
Power: 210bhp @ 6000rpm
Torque: 203lb/ft @ 3500rpm
Transmission: five-speed manual, rear-wheel drive

Suspension
Front: MacPherson struts, lower A-arm
Rear: trailing arms and torsion bar

Brakes
Front and rear: ventilated discs, Porsche racing calipers

Wheels
Front: 7 x 16in
Rear: 8 x 16in

Tyres
Front: 205/55ZR16
Rear: 225/50ZR16

Dimensions
Length: 4320mm
Wheelbase: 2400mm
Width: 1755mm
Weight: 1180kg

Performance
Maximum speed: 150mph
0–60mph: 6.9 seconds

homologation special which had motorsport dripping from every pore. Le Mans regulations required a minimum of 400 models to be built in order for Porsche to be granted permission to compete in the 1980 event (which they did with some success), and while the road car was given 'only' 210bhp compared to the racer's 350bhp, that still gave the delicate 924 range an awesome star.

The visual impact of the 924 Carrera GT was stunning at the time. By comparison, the toughened Turbo was ripped to shreds in terms of sheer eye-popping quality. A massive air scoop dominated the bonnet, and the ubiquitous late 1970s/early 1980s decal also attracted attention. The distended front and rear arches, which added a hefty 40mm to the track, were probably the most impressive alterations to the traditional 924 shape and would later form the basis for the styling evolution for the 944.

Yes, the Carrera GT certainly had the show, but did it have the go to match? Porsche ensured it did by fitting a larger turbine to the turbocharger, upping boost from 0.65 to 0.75 bar and adding a massive air-to-air intercooler. This latter fed from that huge bonnet scoop and helped reduce temperatures by as much as 45 degrees Celsius. Lighter forged pistons were also utilized, and hardened camshafts were fitted to cope with the extra forces. The result was a healthy 210bhp and 203lb/ft from the blown 2-litre mill.

The Carrera GT also benefited from racing tricks such as a lightened exhaust system which shaved over 20kg off the weight. Allied to the extra power, this helped the car hit 60mph in a shade over six and a half seconds, with a top whack of 150mph – both significantly better than anything the Turbo could manage. Stiffer bushing, a lower ride height and chunkier rear anti-roll bars were added to an already strengthened suspension set-up. With superior traction from 7 x 16in Fuchs alloy wheels, the roadgoing racer was a bit of a bobby-dazzler in the handling department.

That said, when you first get into the car and give it a go, by modern criteria first impressions aren't quite up to the standards you'd expect from such a sporting Porsche. The dog-leg gearbox has a long throw, preventing the driver from really rushing through the ratios. The engine (of VW parentage) sounds a little on the coarse side. And don't expect instant pyrotechnics in the acceleration department: with the bigger turbine taking its time to spool up, the Carrera GT suffers from a large dose of lag. Hit 3000rpm, however, and this 924 really takes off. The firm suspension comes into its own at speed, and the steering, heavy at town pace, springs alive with feedback. You need to keep your wits about you to avoid the turbo suddenly coming on-boost mid-corner, but treat the car with respect and it exhibits superb on-limit poise.

The slightly bland interior, brakes that feel a bit soggy by Porsche's very high standards, and the on–off turbo make the Carrera GT feel its age these days, but let's put things in context. Over two decades ago, this car was dishing out 150mph pace and 30mpg practicality. It looked wild, provided a thrilling drive on road or racetrack, but was practical enough to be used as everyday transport. In fact, in terms of criticism the only real question you can level at Porsche is: why did you build only 400 of these magnificent machines?

THE 928

Fuhrmann believed that the old 911 had only a limited shelf life; it had been around for several years already and was beginning to look like an expensive anachronism. He wanted to take the Porsche brand upmarket with an advanced and refined Grand Tourer. The 928 would break the traditional Porsche air-cooled lineage by offering a water-cooled V8, the company's first. This would be front-mounted, with driven rear wheels providing optimum weight distribution and the kind of predictable chassis balance that would appeal to keen drivers. The car would also offer weight-saving technology, luxury and refinement.

1978 Porsche 928

Engine
Power unit: V8, water-cooled
Capacity: 4474cc
Location: front
Valves: two valves per cylinder
Construction: aluminium alloy
Bore x stroke: 95mm x 78.9mm
Compression ratio: 8.5:1
Fuel system: Bosch K-Jetronic
Power: 240bhp @ 5500rpm
Torque: 268b/ft @ 3600rpm
Transmission: five-speed manual, rear-wheel drive

Suspension
Front: independent, coil springs, wishbones, anti-roll bar
Rear: independent, upper transverse links, lower trailing arms, coil springs, anti-roll bar

Brakes
Front and rear: ventilated discs

Wheels
Front and rear: 7 x 16in

Tyres
Front and rear: 225/50

Dimensions
Length: 4445mm
Wheelbase: 2540mm
Width: 1835mm
Weight: 1450kg

Performance
Maximum speed: 142mph
0–60mph: 8.1 seconds

Above *The S models featured spoilers front and rear to aid aerodynamic performance. The small version could pass unnoticed unless next to a standard 928 (see page 94).*

The Tony Lapine-styled 928 was eventually unveiled at the 1977 Geneva Motor Show. The long, jutting bonnet and curving rear attracted a great deal of praise from the public and the press, and the 928 was voted European Car of the Year in 1978.

After the furore that the 924 had caused at its introduction, due to its bastardized parentage, the 928 was seen as a return to form by Porsche. The oil crisis had subsided and all of a sudden a luxury bruiser seemed a perfectly acceptable sort of car again.

The 928 was a real departure for Porsche, taking it into a whole new marketplace and setting it up as a 'proper' manufacturer, with the entry-level 924, the mid-priced, sporting 911, and the expensive, luxury 928 Grand Tourer at the top of the tree, ready to take on the Jaguar XJS and the Mercedes SL.

Like the 924, the body was a conglomeration of stark, wedgy lines and sumptuous curves. The 928 had no apparent front and rear bumpers, as they were incorporated into plastic nose and tail sections. This not only allowed for a clean design, it also meant that the bodywork could resist deformation in low-speed impacts. Aluminium doors, bonnet and wings were also used to keep the weight down. The interior certainly included plenty of electrical adjustments and leather. There were some neat tricks too, such as the steering wheel and instrument cluster adjusting together for perfect visibility at all times. An air-conditioned glovebox was also available.

The 4474cc water-cooled V8 also used aluminium in the construction of the heads and block. With Bosch fuel injection and a single overhead camshaft per cylinder bank, the 928 had 240bhp – enough for 0–60mph in under seven seconds and 140mph.

The drive train was similar in principle to the 924's, except here the transmission was located ahead of the differential, more like other front-engined rear-drive cars. Suspension was traditional: fully independent front and rear with coil springs and anti-roll bars. The rear featured the special 'Weissach axle', which altered the toe-in of the rear wheel under load, canting the wheel into the turn and reducing the risk of oversteer. American road testers liked the smooth ability of the 928, but European hacks were less enamoured. The impression was that the 928 lacked the fizz and sparkle of the 911, and was too luxurious to be a sports car.

The 928S appeared in 1979 and set about countering criticisms of the 928's performance. It featured spoilers fore and aft to improve the rather lacklustre aerodynamic performance of the car, and engine capacity was increased to 4.7 litres for better driving flexibility and urge. Power swelled noticeably to 300bhp, torque to 284lb/ft. People now agreed that the 928 went like a

Porsche should. For the 1983 model year the previous two incarnations were replaced by one, an enhanced 'S', now with 310bhp and a top speed of 155mph. For real Porsche people, though, there was something missing. That perceived shortcoming was to be rectified with interest by the heavily revised 928 S4 of 1986.

The 928 was already almost a decade old when the S4 was launched to inject new life into the model. Visually, the S4 benefited from a modified nose section and a more considerable rear spoiler. The engine also came in for substantial attention. It was increased in capacity to 4957cc, and employed twin camshafts per cylinder bank and a sixteen-valve head similar to the one fitted to the 944S. The consequent boost in power permitted a 0–60mph time of six seconds and a top speed of 165mph – serious performance.

Evidently not serious enough, however, as the 928 continued to grow old disgracefully. The 928 GT of 1989 had 330bhp, while the last of the line, the GTS, boasted an incredible 350bhp. And all the time the 928 was being refined and improved into an ever more devastating performance car. Good drivers grew to love the 928's ability on demanding roads and its penchant for devouring continents in an afternoon. It pioneered ABS for Porsche and sold a total of 61,000 examples in its production life.

Still that wasn't enough. By the time of its demise in the early 1990s it was incredibly expensive (over £72,000) and had still never fully made amends in the judgment of those demanding Porsche purists. To them it was a luxo-barge, a Mercedes SL with a twist. It wasn't a proper Porsche. Far from usurping the 911, it just went to prove how indispensable the old warhorse was.

MODEL IN FOCUS: 1989 928 S4GT

The S4 had proved a mixed blessing for Porsche. Some loved it, with its proudly-boasted 'Sport Equipment', nifty handling and all-electric interior adjustment. It was a fabulous example of Grand Tourer style. Many of the more dedicated aficionados hated it, though, believing it too soft and fat to be a true sports car. So, in 1989 and prompted mainly by its British distributors, Porsche renamed its latest version the 928 S4GT, and made it a high-performance special. With enhanced capacity, more raunchiness, smooth riding, ultimate reliability and a bagful of tweaks, it offered much. But did it give the Porsche enthusiast what he wanted?

Above The 928 S4 brought improvements in both styling and power. While its luxury interior was little changed from the S, the spoilers were enlarged, the nose restructured and engine performance and capacity increased.

Left Cutaway view of the 928 S4GT. Note the enlarged spoiler and wider wheels.

Opposite page: top and middle The 928 S2 offered slight power and performance increases over the basic S, but remained in production for only a few months following its launch in 1983, being superseded by the S3 and later S4.

This page and opposite In the late 1980s the 928s were beefed up into first a GT and then this GTS version, available from 1991. The eight-cylinder power unit offered increases in both capacity (5397cc) and output (350 bhp), and sleek Nineties styling inside and out. This is a 1994 example of the 928 GTS.

1989 Porsche S4GT

Engine
Power unit: Liquid-cooled V8, dual resonant induction
Capacity: 4957cc
Location: front
Valves: four per cylinder
Construction: lightweight aluminium-alloy
Bore x stroke: 100mm x 78.9mm
Compression ratio: 10.0:1
Fuel system: Bosch LH-Jetronic injection
Power: 320 bhp@6000rpm
Torque: 318lb/ft @3000rpm
Transmission: five-speed manual or automatic, rear-wheel drive

Suspension
Front: Independent, coil springs, double wishbone, anti-roll bar
Rear: Independent, semi-trailing arms, upper transverse links, coil springs, anti-roll bar, Porsche–Weissach geometry

Brakes
Front: Ventilated discs
Rear: Ventilated discs, servo-assist, ABS

Wheels
Front: Cast alloy, 8J x 16in
Rear: Cast alloy, 9J x 16in

Tyres
Front: 225/50ZR
Rear: 245/45ZR

Dimensions
Length: 4450mm
Wheelbase: 2500mm
Width: 2030mm
Weight: 1580kg

Performance
Maximum speed: 163.5mph **0–60mph:** 5.3 seconds

Well, it wasn't great for the urban driver; the commuter and the city slicker should have stuck with their 911s. Pottering about in traffic the S4GT was a dog: the first three gears of the close-ratio transmission were jerky and the clutch a fraction sharp, and the car never felt comfortable until it was given its head. Drivers complained about the design of the gear lever, with its dog-leg first gear position and stiff switching across the H gate. But the top gears were a dream: you could pull away in fifth at 800rpm with barely a protest, and pretty much stay in fourth and fifth throughout on the open highway. The auto version was reported as smoother in the lower gears but, as we all know, automatic transmission in a sports car is a wimp's option and outside the US it wasn't a great seller. Anyway, one of the main selling points of the 928 S4GT was the fraction above the half-second that it shaved from the S4's 0–60 performance (bringing it down to 5.3 seconds), and that didn't happen with the automatic.

The wheels were an inch or so wider than those on the S4, giving great road-holding power – unless you hit a white line. For some reason Porsche specified Bridgestone RE71 unidirectional 245/45s on the rear, which disagree violently with white paint, causing the rear to skid and swerve quite alarmingly at the slightest touch. It gave the model a reputation it didn't truly deserve and one would have expected better from the Porsche designers. The tyres were even worse on concrete roads, creating a great hum that almost drowned out the engine, and with the hint of oversteer it wasn't always a cinch to drive, particularly in wet weather. One wondered why Porsche had tinkered with this area at all – the wheel set-up for the S4 had given few problems.

That said, the 928 S4GT had many good points, particularly compared with its S4 predecessor. Its suspension was stiffened by ten per cent and given sport model shocks, providing a firm and predictable ride at speed, although again it wasn't great over pot-holed city roads. Its already proven 32-valve all-alloy V8 was tweaked and given higher-profile cams, a modified EMU, and the exhaust system switched to twin tailpipes. Its reported power

and torque were unchanged from the basic S4, but once past 4000rpm the difference was plain. It is unbelievably, stupendously fast – but not in a wild, uncontrollable way, rather a quiet but bullet-fast progression. It would pull happily in fifth from 500 to 6750rpm with barely a bark, and one can easily forget to check the speedometer while marvelling at its grace. Off the public highway and on a race-prepared track it will easily top its reported maximum of 163.5 mph, with 170 easily achievable on a straight flat surface.

Inside, for those who worry about such things, while maintaining most of the interior layout of its predecessor – including the stylish and well-designed dash and instrument panels – the S4GT thankfully ditched the S4's all-electric adjustment system, which was prone to problems and was always more of a toy than anything else. It gained air-conditioning and sports seats, making it the ideal, comfortable car for long-distance speedy motorway driving.

The Club Sport or CS was essentially the same car under the bonnet, but stripped of its comfort items and soundproofing (mainly to reduce weight and make it appear more sporty) and with a lightweight air-con unit. It proved particularly popular in Germany and other countries in mainland Europe, despite its deafening engine noise in the back-to-basics cabin. It didn't appeal to the comfort-loving British though, who had, after all, inspired the development of the GT. That model was, and remains, a rather British hybrid of style, comfort and speed – one on which those who drive it cannot entirely agree: it either works wonderfully or just doesn't quite cut it as a Porsche. However, being limited-edition, the remaining GTs – those that avoided the white lines – now have great rarity value and are highly prized by collectors.

1982 Porsche 944

Engine
Power unit: four-cylinder, in-line, eight-valve head
Capacity: 2479cc
Location: front
Valves: two valves per cylinder
Construction: aluminium alloy
Bore x stroke: 100mm x 78.9mm
Compression ratio: 10.9:1
Fuel system: DME electronic fuel injection
Power: 163bhp @ 5800rpm
Torque: 151lb/ft @ 3000rpm
Transmission: five-speed manual, rear-wheel drive

Suspension
Front: independent MacPherson struts with coil springs, lower wishbones, anti-roll bar

Rear: independent semi-trailing arms, transverse torsion bars, telescopic dampers, anti-roll bar

Brakes
Front and rear: ventilated discs

Wheels
Front and rear: 7J x 15in

Tyres
Front and rear: 215/60

Dimensions
Length: 4213mm
Wheelbase: 2400mm
Width: 1735mm
Weight: 1180kg

Performance
Maximum speed: 131mph
0–60mph: 8.4 seconds

Below The 944 in the Porsche design shop. Bred to take over the ailing 924 market, it borrowed much from the old model, and became a real hit in Turbo form.

THE 944

Even the cynics would have to agree that the 924 had sold in impressive numbers. However, as the 1970s discoed to an end, the demand for the entry-level Porsche was ebbing away. New head man Peter Schutz needed to find a way to rekindle the fire, and it wasn't long before he found it.

At that time, Porsche was developing a new engine for the 924 Turbo body shell. It wasn't practical to develop a V6, and a straight-six wouldn't fit in the engine bay, so a new in-line four was developed, basically by using one of the cylinder banks from the 928. The result was a 2479cc all-aluminium mill which addressed the 924's inherent lack of refinement by using two counter-rotating balancer shafts to counteract secondary forces and vibration.

Schutz saw the potential of the new project but opted to utilize the styling of the fat-arched Carrera GT homologation special. It was hoped the butch new sports car, with over 160bhp and a top speed of around 135mph, would be considered a proper Porsche and not be undermined by its VW/Audi parentage, as had happened to the 924. That said, the 944 used an Audi five-speed gearbox as an integral part of the transaxle, with the same tubular backbone separating it from the engine. It was an identical set-up to the 924 Turbo. Suspension, too, was fundamentally similar to the outgoing model, although updated and upgraded, while the brakes came from the Carrera GT. Even the interior was lifted straight from the outgoing model. This was redressed in 1985, however. With the launch of the new Turbo model, the whole range got an interior restyle, the so-called 'oval dash' models with larger air-vents and the steering wheel raised by 18mm, creating more space for taller drivers.

When the 220bhp 944 Turbo arrived in 1985 it was an instant hit with the press. Despite taking some flak about the fact that it cost almost the same as a 911, it had the performance to match its big brother with a top speed of around 160mph. The Turbo was also a refined cruiser, with all the luxuries a contemporary GT required. Its body was a smoother design, to reduce drag and improve high-speed noise levels. It also featured impressive underbody aerodynamics for improved stability.

This page *A 1985 example of the 944. The rear end was more boxy than the curvy 928, prompting some to consider it uninspired, but the front was instantly recognizable as a Porsche.*

Opposite page: bottom *Cutaway view of the 944.*

In 1988 the Turbo S appeared on the scene in limited-edition colour schemes and packing a 250bhp punch. Porsche had initially planned to produce only 1000 of these cars to ensure exclusivity, but the company soon realized the car's appeal and by 1989 the mainstream 944 Turbo had been upgraded to 250bhp – a decision which understandably irritated a lot of S buyers.

By the late 1980s Porsche was struggling again, especially in the US, where increasing cut-price competition from the Far East, as well as extremely unhelpful currency exchange rates, were making things extremely tough all round. Porsche did what it always has done in such situations: it made a better car. The S2 of 1989 was an evolution of the sixteen-valve 944S which first appeared in 1986. The 190bhp S had used one bank of cylinders from the new 5-litre 928, but it hadn't really worked, lacking the sparkle its specification suggested. The S2 was to change that. It took the sleeker, low-drag bodywork of the Turbo and upped its engine capacity to three litres. Power swelled to 211bhp and, more importantly, torque topped 207lb/ft.

Boasting a cooling system developed from the TAG Formula One programme, stiffer anti-roll bars, the superb brakes from the 250bhp Turbo and sixteen-inch alloy wheels, the S2 had the ability to match its looks. It was a full second quicker to 60mph than the 2.7-litre eight-valve entry-level 944, and capable of almost 150mph. Maybe it couldn't match the outright pace of the Turbo, but with the chassis revisions and extra capacity, the S2 was a sweeter drive. Many

Above and top right *The 2.5-litre 944S arrived after the first Turbos in 1986–7 and was an amalgam of current Porsche technology. It took the basic engine block from the standard 944, the 16-valve head from one half of the 928 S4's V8, and some nifty electronics from the 944 Turbo.*

Bottom right *The S2 followed in 1989, with a new 3-litre engine and revisions to the braking and cooling systems, as well as some overall restyling.*

preferred the more linear, gutsy delivery of the big-four, and if that wasn't enough to convince you, perhaps the £7,000 price difference would.

The S2 Cabriolet appeared soon after the coupé, although the first 944 drop-top had been seen in the form of a design study at the Frankfurt Motor Show in 1985. It had taken nearly five years for the American Sunroof Company (who had secured the commission to build the soft top) to get its new factory operational. With the top in place, getting in and out of the car demanded some degree of agility, and visibility was compromised, but no matter: roof down,

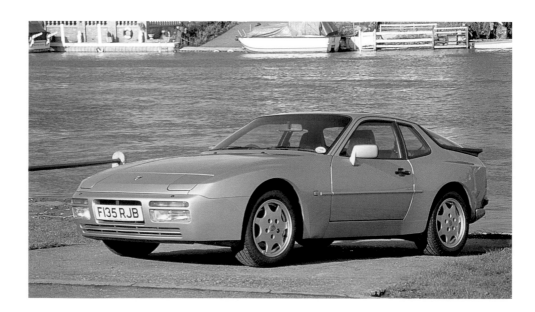

the Cabriolet was a gorgeous machine. The slightly ageing rear-quarter aspect of the coupé, so reminiscent of the 924, was much improved by the flatter rear deck, which accentuated the muscular haunches. A beefed-up floorpan and door pillars reduced flex, and although the Cabriolet lacked practicality, it still found buyers.

In 1991, with the launch of the 968 just round the corner, Porsche offered some attractive run-out deals, and the UK got one of the finest in the form of the SE. For about £2000 more than the S2, it featured lowered suspension, loads of toys and interior upgrades, and a tweaked 225bhp engine. It was a fine way to check out.

MODEL IN FOCUS: 944 TURBO

The 944 Turbo was never the sales success Porsche had hoped it would be, mainly because when it was launched in 1985 its £25,000 price tag put it in the same financial bracket as a 911, yet traditional Porsche buyers still looked upon the 944 as a poor relation, as had been the case with the 924 Turbo seven years earlier. Pity. The 944 was a real hit with the motoring press, who loved its combination of refinement, performance and sublime handling. And in terms of raw performance it was the equal of the 3.2-litre 911 Carrera. With, in its post-1988 guise, 250bhp, it could post a sub-six-second 0–60mph time and reach a top speed of over 160mph. That's why it remains one of the greatest Porsches, even if it was never one of the most loved.

Aerodynamics played a big part in the 944 Turbo's stunning performance. Its sleek lines and integrated front bumper combined with panels beneath the engine bay to provide a cleaner air flow beneath the car at speed. Meanwhile, a rear diffuser assembly drew air out smoothly and cooled the petrol tank and gearbox. The windscreen was bonded in and the fitting was super-flush; even the headlamp and windscreen washer jets were lower profile. The result was superb aerodynamic efficiency, a higher top speed and noticeably less wind and noise intrusion.

Above Always popular: the cabriolet version of the 1990 944. Without the raked rear window the car looked less like the 924 and it sold extremely well.

1987 Porsche 944 Turbo

Engine

Power unit: straight four-cylinder, in-line
Capacity: 2479cc
Location: front
Valves: two valves per cylinder
Construction: aluminium alloy
Bore x stroke: 100mm x 78.9mm
Compression ratio: 8.0:1
Fuel system: Bosch L-jetronic injection
Power: 220bhp @ 5800rpm
Torque: 243lb/ft @ 3500rpm
Transmission: five-speed manual, rear-wheel drive, limited-slip differential

Suspension

Front: independent MacPherson struts with coil springs, lower wishbones, anti-roll bar
Rear: independent semi-trailing arms, transverse torsion bars, anti-roll bar

Brakes

Front: ventilated discs
Rear: plain discs, servo assisted, ABS

Wheels

Front: 7J x 16in
Rear: 8J x 16in

Tyres

Front: 205/55VR
Rear: 225/50VR

Dimensions

Length: 4230mm
Wheelbase: 2400mm
Width: 1735mm
Weight: 1260kg

Performance

Maximum speed: 150.8mph
0–60mph: 5.9 seconds

This latter aspect was actually quite important, because the 944 Turbo played the luxury card just as strongly as the performance card. In fact, 65 per cent of its 100kg weight increase over a stock 944 could be attributed to specification increases. Electrically adjustable Recaro seats, electric sunroof and automatic climate control were all standard fittings.

The 944 Turbo benefited from the many lessons learned during the brief life of its spiritual cousin the 924 Carrera GT. Porsche also claimed to have virtually eliminated turbo-lag by electronically controlling the turbo wastegate, and there was no longer the 'sonic boom' of power shift at the onset of full boost, which had previously caught many an inexperienced driver unawares. Likewise, many other components were revised to cope with the superior output of the force-induced 2.7-litre unit. The clutch grew in diameter and the gearbox was strengthened, and though the stock suspension configuration was carried over, the shocks were stiffer and the anti-roll bar beefed up. Wider, lower-profile 205-section tyres gave better road-holding, particularly on dry roads, and although they also resulted in greater road noise the ride was smooth and those who had previously driven the 924 Turbos and Carreras found it much improved. The initial understeer noted with the basic 944 evened out better than the standard model; here was none of the disquieting oversteer found in previous models, and any tailslide was smooth and controllable. Crosswinds were a different matter though: with its improved aerodynamics and weight change a sideswipe from even a stiff breeze was noticeable at speed, and with the very light steering this could be unnerving the first few times out.

This page *A typical first-generation 944 Turbo, this example dates from 1986 and clearly demonstrates the model's visual appeal.*

Opposite page *Cutaway view of the 944 Turbo, as launched in 1985. Note the flatter front, added to improve aerodynamic efficiency.*

Overall, the Turbo was undeniably beautiful – possibly the best-looking sports coupé ever – despite its departure from Porsche tradition in many of its features. Its minor flaws amount to no more than nit-picking: and its up-to-date comfort features, including air con, fully electrically-adjustable part-leather seats and removable sunroof, ensure it will continue to be a classic in demand for many years to come.

THE 968

At the start of the 1990s Porsche was looking a little bit fragile. The 911 was still going, but the 944 had died in the convulsions suffered by the world economy following 1987's stock market crash. The 928 limped on, but this £70,000 dinosaur was incapable of saving the company. Even the motor-racing scene, so often the saving grace for Porsche, was producing bad news:

both the high-profile Arrows Formula One and Indy Car projects were sources of more embarrassment than glory.

Porsche needed a new model and quickly, a car that was affordable enough to lure in large numbers of new buyers but wouldn't further tarnish an already battered image. To achieve this, Porsche would have to outperform the opposition, look good and not drain people's pockets. The problem was that Porsche simply did not have the cashflow available to fund the development of an all-new model, so what the public got when the 968 hit the streets in mid-1991 was a car described somewhat oddly as '80 per cent new'. The motoring press certainly didn't buy that particular gem. What Porsche had clearly done was revamp the 944 – a policy, according to group development director Paul Hensler, of evolution, not revolution.

The 968 carried over the big 3-litre four-cylinder engine from the 944, but with significant improvements. In an attempt to prove that a proper sports car could have a four-cylinder powerplant the first step was to up the power, and a number of weight-saving measures such as the use of lightened, forged pistons and con-rods allowed the rev limit to be increased to 6200rpm from 5800rpm. A heavily revised inlet manifold was designed, and Porsche developed a variable-cam timing device (VarioCam) to enable better low-rev torque without compromising top-end power. Finally, a free-flowing (and lovely sounding) exhaust system was put in place to give the four a suitably sporty soundtrack. The resulting outputs were 240bhp and 225lb/ft of twisting power – enough, in conjunction with the six-speed manual transmission, to reach 60mph in 6.2 seconds and top 156mph.

The DNA of the 944 was still clearly visible in the 968, but numerous styling tweaks helped freshen and modernize the shape. Its 'corporate' face, more in line with the 928 and 911 models, did away with the 944's much-copied pop-up headlamps. The 968's were permanently on view, and they retracted by folding backwards into the wing. The drag coefficient suffered slightly to incorporate the new mechanism, but by using flexible polyurethane front and rear panels, practicality was improved and parking dings much reduced. If the frontal aspect raised a few questions, though, few argued that the pert, tidy rear was anything but a big step forward: it was clean, stylish, modern and uncluttered. The interior and luggage space was instantly recognizable to late-model 944 owners, save for the odd read-out and the airbagged wheel, as it was lifted almost unaltered. That meant solid build and functional ergonomics, but something of a sombre atmosphere.

The early star of a range that singularly refused to excite the press was the Cabriolet. Hood down, the topless 968 was, and indeed is, one of the most attractive-looking vehicles on the roads, the cleaned-up profile really suiting the drop top stance.

Shortly afterwards, in 1993, Porsche announced a truly exciting 968 – the Club Sport (see page 109), which remains a classic. A few months later Porsche unleashed the most potent 968 of them all. The Turbo S was a fiendishly expensive, strictly limited homologation special created to allow Porsche to compete in a new German GT race series. Built on a special production line at Porsche's Weissach research centre, the Turbo S used the 944 Turbo's eight-valve head and a water-cooled KKK

1992 Porsche 968

Engine
Power unit: four-cylinder, in-line, sixteen-valve head
Capacity: 2990cc
Location: front
Valves: four valves per cylinder
Construction: light alloy
Bore x stroke: 104mm x 88mm
Compression ratio: 11.0:1
Fuel system: DME digital fuel injection
Power: 240bhp @ 6200rpm
Torque: 225lb/ft @ 4100rpm
Transmission: six-speed manual, rear-wheel drive

Suspension
Front: independent MacPherson struts with coil springs, lower wishbones, anti-roll bar
Rear: independent semi-trailing arms, transverse torsion bars, telescopic dampers, anti-roll bar

Brakes
Front and rear: ventilated discs, ABS

Wheels
Front: 7 x 16in
Rear: 8 x 16in

Tyres
Front: 205/55
Rear: 225/50

Dimensions
Length: 4320mm
Wheelbase: 2400mm
Width: 1735mm
Height: 1275mm
Weight: 1370kg

Performance
Maximum speed: 156mph
0–60mph: 6.5 seconds

Left Cutaway view of the 968 as it appeared in 1992, incorporating the VarioCam system.

Opposite page: top A 1993 model of the 968 on show. Built to rescue the company from the worldwide recession, the model never gained public affection and disappeared quietly in 1995.

Opposite page: bottom The interior of the 968 differed little from that of the recent 944s.

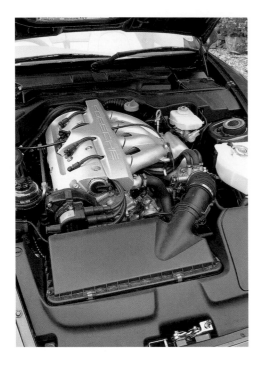

Above and top right *The 968 Cabriolet of 1993 demonstrates that the 968 shape worked well in topless form.*

Right *The limited-edition Turbo S of 1994, built to allow Porsche to qualify for GT racing in its home country, has developed an enthusiastic fan base worldwide and is highly collectible.*

Opposite page *The 1994 968 Sport, a special that adopted enhancements from the Club Sport and packaged them into the basic 968 with a few luxury extras to tempt the British buyer.*

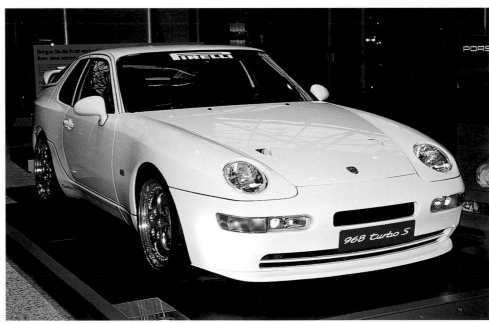

blower running at 1-bar boost. This was enough for 305bhp and a monster 369lb/ft of torque; the Turbo S could top 175mph, and has become a cult car.

Perhaps the best of the 968s, though, was the UK-only Sport. British buyers were put out at how cheap 968s were in the US, but wanted less spartan accommodation than the bargain-basement Club Sport. The Sport kept the CS's chassis upgrades but added a few toys, yet was still £5,500 cheaper than a standard-specification 968.

Sadly for the 968, the recession lingered on and on and the 968 never returned the sort of sales figures that would warrant its survival. It had serious shortcomings. The 944's chassis tooling was still being used and panel gaps of 7mm were double the industry standard – simply unacceptable for a quality marque. Also, many of the 968's components and technologies

were developed from the 1970s, and the car simply wasn't as fresh as it looked. By the middle of 1995, Porsche had pulled the plug.

MODEL IN FOCUS: THE 968 CLUB SPORT

The Club Sport, following a tradition set with the celebrated 911 Carrera CS and S4 CS models (see earlier), was designed to be a stripped down, all-out racer – one that would appeal to those who fancied a more sporty, less comfort-driven look and feel – and those with a lower budget. In fact, it was to the 968 what the 911 RS America was to the 911 Carrera: totally stripped of the standard 968's electric gizmos and luxuries, it had race seats, no rear bench, lower suspension and a price tag far lower than any other Porsche, or for that matter many of its direct competitors of the time. Add to this its wild paint job and snazzy decals, plus optional fancies like body-coloured wheels, and the Club Sport was no shrinking violet. Crucially, it had the ability to back up its looks, wowing road testers with its sublime handling and undiluted driving pleasure, and was judged best-handling car of 1993 by *Autocar and Motor* magazine. Judging by the internet web sites that celebrate it today, it particularly appealed to the Japanese and those Americans who wanted it for highway burns, but its basic, no-nonsense interior never particularly appealed to the British Porsche market, who demanded their own version, the 968 Sport, a less spartan but equally affordable model.

The 968 CS was powered by the last water-cooled four-cylinder front-mounted engine that Porsche would build. It remains a classic, and a rare enough one at that: only 1923 were ever made and somewhat fewer than that are still in driveable condition.

1993 Porsche 968 Club Sport

Engine
Power unit: four-cylinder, in-line, sixteen-valve, KKK turbocharger
Capacity: 2990cc
Location: front
Valves: four valves per cylinder
Construction: light alloy
Bore x stroke: 104mm x 88mm
Compression ratio: 7.5:1
Fuel system: Sequential multi-port, DME digital fuel injection
Power: 305bhp @ 5400rpm
Torque: 369lb/ft @ 3000rpm
Transmission: six-speed manual, rear-wheel drive, 75% limited slip differential under power

Suspension
Front: independent MacPherson struts with springs, lower control arms, anti-roll bar
Rear: independent semi-trailing arms, transverse torsion bars, anti-roll bar

Brakes
Front and rear: four-pot aluminium alloy fixed calipers, ventilated and cross-drilled discs, ABS

Wheels
Front: Speedline alloy, 8 x 17in
Rear: Speedline alloy, 10 x 17in

Tyres
Front: 225/45
Rear: 255/40

Dimensions
Length: 4341mm
Wheelbase: 2400mm
Width: 1735mm
Height: 1275mm
Weight: 1302kg

Performance
Maximum speed: 176mph
0–60mph: 4.5 seconds

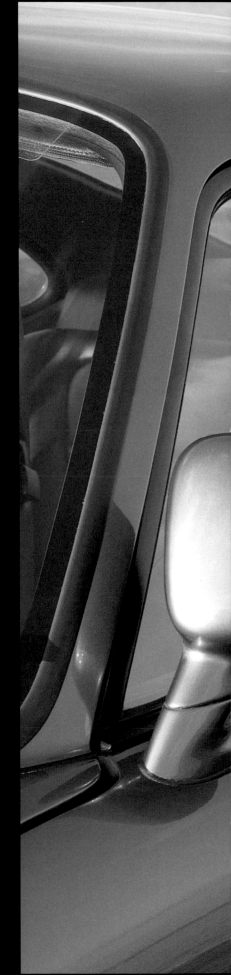

chapter
seven

The
special
911s

There has never been any doubt that Porsche has created special automobiles. From the first 356 Speedsters of the 1950s, through the early 911s of the 1960s and 1970s to the supercar-slaying 911 Turbos of the 1980s, Porsche has always managed to turn out road cars which offer that little something over and above the norm.

Porsche's roots are firmly planted in motorsport. From Ferdinand Porsche's first engineering exploits through to sixteen outright victories at the legendary 24 Heures du Mans, the Stuttgart firm has found the art of winning on the track as straightforward as building road-winning cars. Porsche has combined its motorsport requirements and successes with the demands from its ever loyal customer base to its advantage, producing ever more extreme and highly focused road cars that capture the essence of the firm's on-track exploits. These are the cars for people who find regular Porsches too run-of-the-mill. These are the ultimate Porsches. The limited-run models, the recaptured machines that are more familiar with the pit lane than your high-street petrol station forecourt. These are the true race cars for the road, the Porsches that offer the purest, least diluted driving experience. These are the specials.

THE 959

Previous page A star of road and track, the 959 had shattering performance and style.

Below Cutaway view of the 959 supercar. Designed at Weissach specifically for Group B racing it offered 0–60 in a stunning 3.6 seconds.

The 959 will go down in history as the ultimate incarnation of the 911. It was the leanest, most powerful (until today's 996 generation GT2, that is) and technologically advanced supercar ever to drive out of the Stuttgart gates.

Premièred at the 1983 Frankfurt Motor Show, the 959 was originally showcased as a design study for Porsche's entry into Group B motorsport competition, which would include both Le Mans racers and a rally car to tackle the gruelling Paris–Dakar desert race. At the time, and as is still the case today, to enable the 959 to be eligible for Group B competition Porsche would

have to build at least 200 roadgoing examples of the model for homologation purposes. However, rather than follow the same route as its competitors and build a few hundred competition cars totally unsuited to the road, Porsche opted to take the opportunity to show off new technology. There was also the small matter of the 959 being the first production car to reach 200mph, a statistic which would allow Porsche to get one up on its closest rival, Ferrari.

But what should have been a momentous occasion for Porsche turned out to be a bit of a damp squib. Industrial action throughout Germany during the car's development period slowed down the project, as did the complexity of the car itself, with which even Porsche's highly experienced engineers were having trouble coming to terms. On top of this came a series of tragic accidents during rounds of the World Rally Championship involving Group B machines such as the Lancia Delta S4 and Ford RS200. This meant that before the 959 was readied

for competition Group B rallying had been banished to the history books. All was not lost in terms of the 959's rallying aspirations, though, as René Metge scored an outright victory at the 1986 Paris–Dakar.

The roadgoing 959 was an exceptional piece of kit. The car's 911esque shape was formed after extensive work in the wind tunnel to produce a shape which would not only maximize the car's aerodynamics but also minimize lift at high speed. With the exception of the aluminium doors and bonnet, the 959's body was put together using a combination of deformable PUR-RIMM plastics (for the nose) and Kevlar reinforced glass fibre (with which the rest of the car's panels were constructed), with production methods taken from the aviation industry.

Top *The roadgoing 959 was chock-full of technological innovation, including the bodyshell, which owed much to aircraft design.*

Above *A cutaway of the 959 showing the flat-six engine. This featured water-cooled cylinder heads and turbos, but the standard Porsche air cooling for the engine block.*

Porsche 959

Engine

Power unit: six-cylinder, horizontally opposed
Capacity: 2850cc
Location: rear
Construction: aluminium alloy
Bore x stroke: 95mm x 67mm
Compression ratio: 8.3:1
Fuel system: twin two-stage turbo-chargers, air-to-air intercooler, water-cooled, Bosch Motronic programmed injection and ignition
Power: 450bhp @ 6500rpm
Torque: 369lb/ft @ 5500rpm
Transmission: six-speed manual, four-wheel drive

Suspension

Front: double wishbones, coil springs, twin Bilstein dampers per wheel, adjustable ride height, anti-roll bar
Rear: double wishbones, coil springs, twin Bilstein dampers per wheel, adjustable ride height, anti-roll bar

Brakes

Front: 322mm ventilated discs, ABS
Rear: 304mm ventilated discs, ABS

Wheels

Front: magnesium alloy, 8J x 17in
Rear: magnesium alloy, 9J x 17in

Tyres

Front: 235/45VR17
Rear: 255/40VR17

Dimensions

Length: 4260mm
Wheelbase: 2272mm
Width: 1840mm
Weight: 1450kg

Performance

Maximum speed: 197mph
0–60mph: 3.9 seconds

Beneath the 959's shell was a technical tour de force. Porsche had insisted that the 959 should feature a four-wheel-drive transmission, and this it duly did. Rather than take an off-the-shelf four-wheel-drive transmission from the likes of Audi, though, Porsche took the decision to develop a system that could not only provide the natural benefits of four-wheel drive, such as traction, but which could also deal with the tougher problems of four-wheel-drive systems when pushed to the limit. These problems included retaining good steering responses and feedback while driving the front wheels, and, crucially, ensuring that the front and rear axles distributed the correct levels of torque and power under acceleration, on differing surfaces and under varying conditions.

Naturally, Porsche developed a four-wheel-drive transmission that was beautifully complex and devastatingly effective. The rear wheels were driven directly from the six-speed manual gearbox via a conventional differential. The gearbox also incorporated an output shaft to the front differential, which housed the Porsche Control Clutch (PSK). This multi-plate clutch, with its seven steel plates bathed in oil, functioned in a similar fashion to a more conventional differential in that when any slippage was detected between the front and rear axles, pressure was applied to the plates to distribute the torque to the axle with the least slippage. However, there was much more to the 959's transmission than just a series of mechanical differentials. A number of sensors located throughout the car's chassis measured wheel speed and slip, engine revs and steering input, and from these recordings the control unit could determine how much torque should be split between the two axles. Under normal driving conditions this would mean a 40–60 front–rear split, but under hard acceleration this would revert to a 20–80 split. The driver could also select, via a dashboard-mounted switch, one of four programmes to suit different conditions: dry, wet, snow and lock. The latter enabled the driver to lock a differential should he try to drive off in thick snow.

The 959's transmission was a complex and costly development for Porsche, but at the same time an essential one, for the 959's engine was to be just as special. Located in the tail, the flat-six engine was a huge leap forward in terms of development for Porsche. The cylinder heads were water-cooled and had their very own cooling system, with radiators mounted behind the rear wheels, but the engine's aluminium block was air-cooled. They also featured four valves per head, with sodium-filled exhaust valves. The engine con-rods were manufactured from titanium and the engine relied on a dry-sump oil lubrication. The two KKK turbochargers were water-cooled and featured an air-to-air intercooler, and were combined to work in a two-stage charging system which reduced turbo lag and provided the engine with sharper throttle responses. With the very latest Bosch Motronic management system installed as well, the 959 was virtually unbeatable. Maximum power for the road car was 450bhp produced at 6500rpm, with 369lb/ft of torque available at 5500rpm. The 0–60mph dash was dismissed in 3.9 seconds, and the 959's maximum speed was an eye-watering 197mph. With their race-bred F40, Ferrari would go just two miles an hour quicker than that.

The 959's double-wishbone suspension and coil spring set-up was a direct derivative of Porsche's racing machines, and with two dampers per wheel and automatic self-levelling, the

Above A view of the 959 cabin.

Opposite
Top *A rear shot of the 959 showing its distinctive spoiler and the full-width light bar proclaiming the maker's name.*
Bottom *The compact but powerful engine of the 959.*

lucky 959 driver could always be assured of complete control. Naturally, Porsche developed the 959's brakes from everything it had learned from the track as well. Massive 322mm (front) and 304mm (rear) ventilated discs were clamped with powerful four-piston calipers. A newly developed Porsche-WABCO anti-locking braking system was also incorporated, the first of its kind to be fitted to a Porsche. Other technological breakthroughs included tyre pressure monitors for each of the four magnesium alloy wheels.

At £155,000, the 959 came with a price tag to go with its supercar status. With just 200 examples produced in a mixture of Comfort and Sport models – the latter with no air conditioning, rear seats or the sophisticated ride height adjustable suspension – the 959 was made available only to existing Porsche customers (those unlikely to have been 924 Lux customers!), and the majority headed straight for private collections, only seeing the light of day when the supercar speculator market crashed in the mid-1990s. For the lucky few who drove the 959

Above *A competition-prepared 959. Originally designed for racing, and winner of the 1986 Paris–Dakar rally, the 959 was ideal for many competitive series – if you could afford one. Note the rollcage, visible around the door opening.*

Opposite page *The 'RS' designation has a proud history. Here is a 1984 Carrera 911 RS, race-prepared for Group 8 competition.*

when new, and for those who have subsequently driven an example in recent years, it remains one of the Porsche driving experiences, its phenomenal power delivery, athletic poise and superb road-holding yielding one of the most focused and involved drives around. The Ferrari F40 might have stolen the limelight, and McLaren's all-conquering F1 might have grabbed the headlines, but the Porsche 959 still has a place in every enthusiast's heart as the most accomplished all-round supercar that has ever terrorized the tarmac.

THE 911 (964) RS

The 3.6-litre Carrera RS was virtually a road-legal version of the original Carrera 'Cup' racer. Manufactured and produced under FISA (motorsport's governing body) homologation rules, the RS was available in two specifications: a sporting 'base' model and a more comfort-orientated 'Touring' model.

As with the original 1973 2.7 RS, the 964 RS's specification was aimed fairly and squarely at the race track. Its air-cooled 3.6-litre flat-six was taken from the regular Carrera 2, but was blueprinted and fitted with a freer-breathing air filter and exhaust system, which resulted in a 15bhp power increase to 260bhp. The 964 RS also adopted the 'Cup' racing car's modified five-speed gearbox, which featured taller first and second gears, and a limited-slip differential taken from the then current 911 Turbo.

Adjustable anti-roll bars and a 40mm drop in the car's ride height formed part of the RS package, and together with a set of 17in Cup design magnesium alloy wheels, the 964 RS was every part a racer.

There was no underbody protection or soundproofing and no rear seats; the car's interior trim was also limited to plain cloth, with two Recaro seats taking pride of place. The roll cage was deleted from the standard equipment list, but it could of course be selected as an option from the Weissach factory. In Touring trim the RS gained underbody protection and

soundproofing, but still there were no rear seats, and it weighed in at 100kg less than a regular Carrera 2. In race trim, the RS was a full 150kg lighter than the standard car.

The 964 RS took the undiluted Porsche driving experience to new limits. Its air-cooled motor thrived on revs, with hair-trigger throttle responses urging the driver to extract every last one of those eager horses from the engine. Sharpness is the best word to sum up the 964 RS, because along with that willing engine came a suspension and steering set-up to die for. With a firmer ride than the standard Carrera 2, the 964 RS provided levels of feedback that had been absent from the 911 since the days of the original 2.7 RS. Sitting snugly in those hip-hugging Recaro seats, the driver felt at one with the car, a part of every suspension movement, every crest in the road, every rise and fall of the path ahead. Coupled with the direct steering, this RS could change direction with the slightest turn of lock while feeding back every last nugget of information from the front wheels.

When new, the RS was perhaps a little too raw for the enthusiasts. Its spartan cabin was a touch too crude, the suspension too harsh when compared with its contemporaries, the cabin noise – amplified by the lack of sound deadening – too grating for many. Today, though, of all the 911s the 964 RS is the model for which the enthusiasts chomp at the bit should they be lucky enough to be offered a chance to get behind the wheel. With sports cars becoming ever more sanitized and diluted, the RS remains a pure driving machine. That it has taken ten years for the 964 RS to firmly establish its niche goes to show that once again Porsche had produced a car the world wasn't quite ready for.

Porsche 911 (964) RS

Engine
Power unit: six-cylinder, horizontally opposed, air-cooled
Capacity: 3600cc
Location: rear
Construction: aluminium alloy
Bore x stroke: 100mm x 76.4mm
Compression ratio: 11.8:1
Fuel system: Bosch sequential fuel injection and ignition
Power: 260bhp @ 6100rpm
Torque: 240lb/ft @ 4800rpm
Transmission: five-speed manual, rear-wheel drive

Suspension
Front: MacPherson struts, coil springs, anti-roll bar
Rear: semi-trailing arm, coil springs, anti-roll bar

Brakes
Front: 322mm ventilated discs, four-piston calipers, ABS
Rear: 299mm ventilated discs, two-piston calipers, ABS

Wheels
Front: magnesium alloy, 7.5J x 17in
Rear: magnesium alloy, 9J x 17in

Tyres
Front: 205/50ZR17
Rear: 255/40VR17

Dimensions
Length: 4250mm
Wheelbase: 2271mm
Width: 1651mm
Weight: 1230kg

Performance
Maximum speed: 162mph
0–60mph: 5.3 seconds

Above *The 993 Carrera Turbo 4 of 1995. This was a true supercar, offering astounding power, acceleration and straight-line performance.*

THE 911 (993) TURBO 4

The Porsche 911 line-up would not be complete without a 911 Turbo, and with the 993 generation Turbo Porsche took its supercar to the next level. With this, the first four-wheel-drive 911 Turbo, Porsche made a conscious decision to tackle the supercar market head-on, knowing it would be up against Ferrari with its sublime F355 and Lamborghini with its monstrous Diablo, both models playing very effectively on passion, history and sheer brute force. Porsche went for precision.

Arriving in 1995, the 911 Turbo was equipped with a technical specification that almost defied belief. Here was a car that, according to the paperwork, produced 408bhp from its twin KKK turbocharged 3.6-litre flat-six air-cooled engine, and there was almost as much torque, with 398lb/ft available with a full stretch of the right foot. Given this kind of horsepower, and the four-wheel-drive transmission from the regular Carrera 4, there was going to be very little doubt surrounding this 911 Turbo's claimed performance: 0–60mph in just four and a half seconds, and 180mph at top whack. The 911 Turbo had truly come of age.

With such devastating power, stupendous grip and phenomenal brakes that were capable of hauling it from 100mph to a standstill in an incredible 3.8 seconds, the 993 generation Turbo left nothing and no one wanting. It possessed an uncanny ability to stay clean and true when directed into a corner with the throttle floored, with not a hint of wild oversteer or white-knuckle understeer; furthermore, the 993 Turbo would just grip and go without the slightest trace of a tyre chirp from any of its four driven wheels.

A turbocharged 911's heart has always been its engine, and with the 993 model it was no different. Featuring two KKK K16 turbochargers, the flat-six motor was controlled by a Bosch

5.2 Motronic engine management system and cooled with two massive air-to-air intercoolers. The engine management's ability to control both air flow and the turbo-chargers' wastegates enabled the engine's compression ratio to be reliably raised to 8.1:1 from 7.5:1, as used on the previous-generation model. This also allowed the engine to run on unleaded fuel and the preferred supercar choice of 98-octane super unleaded. The results, as have already been described, were nothing short of remarkable, and were made even more impressive of course by the Turbo's sophisticated four-wheel-drive system, which happily gave the driver the leeway to extract every last drop of power. The Turbo was also fitted with a six-speed manual gearbox taken from the regular 911 Carrera 4, and drive was split with a 20–80 bias to the rear. A limited slip differential was also fitted, while Porsche automatic brake distribution offered traction control up to 44mph.

As with all 993-generation 911s, the Turbo sported a new multi-link rear suspension which, alongside improving the car's ride and helping to reduce the inherent rear weight bias, allowed for greater control and stability at high speed. And when you consider the speeds this 911 Turbo was capable of, that could only have been a good thing. MacPherson front suspension was once again used, although it was, like the rear, constructed from lighter aluminium materials to help reduce unsprung weight, which in turn improved the car's steering feel and reactions.

Distinguishing the 911 Turbo from its lesser brethren was a body 60mm wider than the regular 911 of the time. The front and rear valances were squared off, and the front bumper also incorporated a larger single opening, with a smaller air duct either side to aid cooling for the brakes. Distinctive lower-edge side skirts ran the length of the car to the wider rear arches, and they in turn supported a further evolution of

Porsche 911 (993) Turbo

Engine
Power unit: six-cylinder, horizontally opposed, air-cooled
Capacity: 3600cc
Location: rear
Construction: aluminium alloy
Bore x stroke: 100mm x 76.4mm
Compression ratio: 8.0:1
Fuel system: Bosch 5.2 Motronic engine management system
Power: 408bhp @ 5750rpm
Torque: 398lb/ft @ 4500rpm
Transmission: six-speed manual, four-wheel drive

Suspension
Front: MacPherson struts, coil springs, anti-roll bar
Rear: multi-link, coil springs, anti-roll bar

Brakes
Front: 322mm ventilated and cross-drilled discs, four-piston calipers, ABS
Rear: 299mm ventilated and cross-drilled discs, four-piston calipers, ABS

Wheels
Front: magnesium alloy, 8J x 17in
Rear: magnesium alloy, 10J x 17in

Tyres
Front: 225/40ZR18
Rear: 285/30VR18

Dimensions
Length: 4245mm
Wheelbase: 2272mm
Width: 1795mm
Weight: 1575kg

Performance
Maximum speed: 180mph
0–60mph: 4.5 seconds

Left A not unfamiliar view of the 993 Turbo 4 – the rear. Wide and low, it featured 10in rear wheels and twin exhausts in addition to the hallmark spoiler.

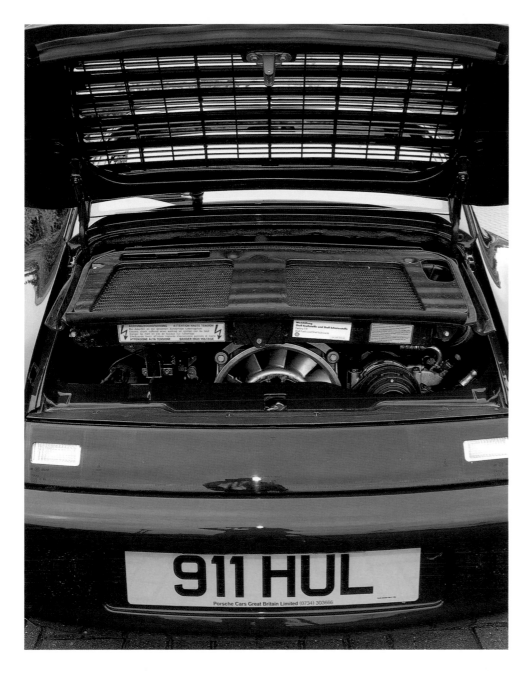

Left *Neat and tidy; the engine compartment of the 993 Turbo with its large grille covering the KKK turbos.*

Above
Top *The front of the 993 Turbo 4 showing its optimal luggage space – well, enough for the laptop at least.*
Bottom *The luxurious interior of this 1995 Turbo 4 was fully kitted out in stylish black leather, reflecting the model's price and status.*

Opposite page *Cutaway view of the 993 Turbo 4. Note the wide shape of the rear, partly due to those enormous wheels, and the new four-wheel drive system.*

the 911's infamous tea-tray rear spoiler design. The final visual tweak came with a set of eight-inch-wide front and ten-inch-wide rear alloy wheels. The overall appearance of the last air-cooled 911 Turbo trod a perfect line between subtlety and brutality. Its squat stance, pumped haunches and smooth edges left you in no doubt that this was a special 911, yet at the same time it could provide you with all the effortless style of a luxury saloon.

The combined beauty, performance and ability of the 993-generation Turbo has ensured its place in the history books. After twenty years of development the 911 had evolved into the most user-friendly supercar money could buy. Whether your aspirations focused on the race-track or a winding country lane on a Sunday afternoon, the 911 Turbo could deliver the goods.

Some say that with the introduction of the water-cooled 911 in 1997 the 911's soul was destroyed. If that is true, then there was no better way for the air-cooled generation to sign off than with the ultimate air-cooled 911, the 993-generation Turbo 4.

Porsche 911 GT1

Engine

Power unit: six-cylinder, horizontally opposed, water-cooled
Capacity: 3164cc
Location: mid-engined
Construction: aluminium alloy
Bore x stroke: 95mm x 74.4mm
Compression ratio: 9.3:1
Fuel system: Bosch 5.2 engine management system
Power: 544bhp @ 7000rpm
Torque: 443lb/ft @ 4250rpm
Transmission: six-speed manual, rear-wheel drive

Suspension

Front and rear: double wishbones, adjustable coil springs and dampers, anti-roll bar

Brakes

Front: 380mm ventilated and cross-drilled discs, eight-piston calipers, Bosch ABS
Rear: 380mm ventilated and cross-drilled discs, four-piston calipers, Bosch ABS

Wheels

Front: three-piece BBS magnesium alloy, 11J x 18in
Rear: three-piece BBS magnesium alloy, 13J x 18in

Tyres

Front: 295/35ZR18
Rear: 335/30ZR18

Dimensions

Length: 4710mm
Wheelbase: 2500mm
Width: 1950mm
Weight: 1250kg

Performance

Maximum speed: 192mph
0–60mph: 3.7 seconds

THE 911 GT1

By 1997 it was clearly apparent that no matter how far the regulations were pushed, if Porsche was to return to winning form at Le Mans and in GT racing around the globe it could no longer rely on an evolution of the production 911. To compete head-on with the likes of McLaren's F1 and the Mercedes CLK-GTR, Porsche needed to develop a car with just one goal in mind: winning. And with a balance sheet looking disgustingly healthy and global sales continuously rising, Porsche needed little encouragement or justification to embark on a project to build a successor to the 959.

The 911 GT1 was designed as an out-and-out racer from the start. Its flat-six engine was rotated through 180 degrees and located amidships in the car's chassis, but crucially ahead of the rear axle for optimum weight distribution. Significantly, the GT1's engine was an evolution of the new water-cooled unit that would appear in the next-generation 911 due to be launched soon after the GT1, although its specification was pure racer. The engine's 3164cc capacity was reached by using the bore and stroke from the previous 962 racers (95mm x 74.4mm), and many of the components of the engine's block were borrowed too. The water-cooled cylinder heads had first been seen on the 959, but the GT1 featured four valves per cylinder and twin camshafts.

Forced induction came courtesy of twin KKK K27 turbochargers, the same units as used in the GT2, but with individual wastegates controlled by a state-of-the-art Bosch 5.2 engine management system. In full Le Mans race specification, maximum power was an exuberant 544bhp produced at 7,000rpm with 443lb/ft of torque produced at 4250rpm, which was transmitted through a six-speed, full synchromesh gearbox complete with a limited slip differential.

The brakes for the GT1 were just as formidable, with 380mm ventilated discs fitted all round, the front discs clamped by eight-piston calipers and

Right The Le Mans Porsche GT1 of 1996. GT1s came second and third at the Sarthe circuit that year.

the rears with four-piston items. The whole system was controlled through a Bosch anti-lock braking system. Three-piece BBS magnesium alloy wheels were fitted, measuring 11J x 18in at the front and 13J x 18in at the rear, and the new model wore steamroller-width 295/35ZR18 tyres at the front and 335/30ZR18 at the rear. The GT1's suspension was suspended from the car's tubular chassis and comprised a traditional racing double-wishbone set-up all round, with horizontally positioned springs and dampers. The front and rear anti-roll bars were infinitely adjustable.

Visually, Porsche went to great lengths to ensure the GT1 looked like a Porsche. The silhouette was clearly that of a 911, with its steel body affixed to an integrated roll cage and side-impact protection shell. The outer panelling of the car's body was manufactured from carbon fibre and formed three core areas: the front nose, which incorporated the front spoiler, the rear engine cover and the rear wing. In true racer style the road cars also featured thinner glass, and the PVC underbody protection was removed.

As you would expect of a true road racer, the GT1's interior was nothing but functional. The two hip-hugging bucket seats were covered in leather, but the three-point safety harness left you under no illusion that this car was anything but racetrack-bred. A bank of instruments faced you, the rev-counter taking pride of place in true Porsche tradition, a speedometer, oil pressure, oil level and oil temperature gauge to either side. Water temperature and fuel level meters were also included. Heating was via a regular variable and adjustable fan, although air-conditioning was available as an option. The interior could also be trimmed in any colour you liked – as long as it was black, that is!

Unlike previous homologation specials, Porsche was required to produce only one road car version of the GT1 under the Le Mans and FIA regulations it

This page One of the few: a privately owned 911 GT1 road car, inside and out. Costing more than the average riverside penthouse, they were strictly for the wealthy collector, despite the spartan, race-designed interior.

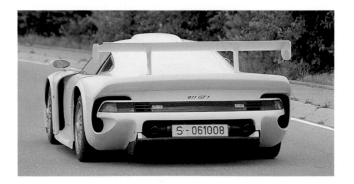

was built to satisfy. However, at a time when serious supercars were back in vogue those few with £650,000 burning a hole in their pocket could order a road-legal version of the 911 GT1 – the ultimate Porsche.

A RIGHT PAIR: THE 993 AND 996 GT2

The 993 and 996 were basically two 911s sharing the same name, yet to the hardcore Porsche enthusiasts they were very different.

The original GT2, based on the 993-generation 911, was a pure motorsport homologation special devised to meet the requirements of the new GT2 class of the IMSA race series in the States, as well as the ADAC Cup Championship in Germany and the BPR Endurance Championship, which embraced classic events such as Le Mans and Daytona. Up until this point Porsche had successfully contested its 3.8 RS and RSR 911s, and these normally aspirated machines had tasted success at every race in which they had competed. With the original GT2, though, Porsche would take the stripped-out, pared-to-the-bone racing concept that extra step.

As the introduction of the twin-turbo four-wheel-drive 911 had been so successful, Porsche took this as a basis for its new street racer. The retention of the twin-turbocharged flat-six engine was never in doubt, but whereas the 911 Turbo 'made do' with 408bhp and 398lb/ft of torque, the GT2's motor was subject to a number of minute changes which saw its power increase to a heady 430bhp at 5750rpm. This was only the beginning of the changes, though: the GT2 made do without the 911 Turbo's sophisticated four-wheel-drive system, or any form of traction control. That's right, this tweaked and lightened 911 special was rear-wheel-drive, with only the driver's willpower and control over his own right foot stopping him from becoming an integral part of the countryside through which he was driving.

Beneath the pumped-up, pop-riveted arches of the GT2 was a chassis that had been seriously tweaked to cope with the car's extra performance. A lower ride height, stiffer springs and dampers, a front strut brace and beefed-up rubber bushes all helped to tighten the GT2's chassis a notch higher than had ever been experienced before. The GT2's brakes came in for some attention too, with 322mm ventilated and cross-drilled discs fitted front and rear, along with four-piston calipers. Hiding these impressive stoppers from view was a set of 9J x 18in and 11J x 18in front and rear Speedline three-piece alloy wheels, which were wrapped in equally impressive rubber of 235/40ZR18 at the front and 285/35ZR18 at the rear.

Accommodating this monster set of alloys were those removable front and rear arches, which when attached to the Turbo body's already pumped-up haunches increased the GT2's width by a full 60mm. As with any racer, the GT2 sported an impressive set of aerodynamic spoilers. The front valance was more aggressive in its styling: along with additional air intakes for cooling the brakes, it featured a pair of lower front-wing spoilers designed to generate additional downforce. The side skirts were taken directly from the Turbo model, but that rear wing could only have been designed for a race car. Featuring two gargantuan air intakes for the engine, the spoiler was a two-tier affair with the top plane adjustable to meet the downforce needs of any particular circuit.

Inside, the GT2 took its cue from the GT1 racer that had gone before it. Stripped out and fitted with only the bare essentials, looks-wise the GT2's interior was a long way from the £130,000 supercar it was. There was no leather, air conditioning or climate control, just a pair of racing seats, a roll cage and racing harnesses.

Immediately the 993 GT2 found a place in the hearts of 911 and Porsche enthusiasts. Its

This page *Bang up to date: the Porsche 911 GT2 of 2001 was even wider than the Turbo 4 but somehow looked less butch, despite its chunky rear spoiler and low front air scoops.*

Opposite page *The unmistakable 911 GT1 road car of 1997 with its distinctive skirted body shape. Just look at the width of those wheels.*

Porsche 911 (993) GT2

Engine
Power unit: six-cylinder, horizontally opposed, air-cooled
Capacity: 3600cc
Location: rear
Construction: aluminium alloy
Bore x stroke: 100mm x 76.4mm
Compression ratio: 8.0:1
Fuel system: Bosch 5.2 engine management system, twin KKK turbochargers
Power: 430bhp @ 5750rpm
Torque: 395lb/ft @ 4500rpm
Transmission: six-speed manual, rear-wheel drive

Suspension
Front: MacPherson struts, adjustable coil springs and dampers, anti-roll bar
Rear: multi-link adjustable coil springs and dampers, anti-roll bar

Brakes
Front and rear: 322mm ventilated and cross-drilled discs, four-piston calipers, ABS

Wheels
Front: three-piece Speedline alloy, 9J x 18in
Rear: three-piece Speedline alloy, 11J x 18in

Tyres
Front: 235/40ZR18
Rear: 285/30ZR18

Dimensions
Length: 4245mm
Wheelbase: 2272mm
Width: 1855mm
Weight: 1290kg

Performance
Maximum speed: 186 mph
0–60mph: 3.7 seconds

Above *The innovative Porsche Ceramic Composite Brake system as used on the GT2.*

phenomenal power and crushing performance (184mph at full stretch, 0–60mph in 3.9 seconds) managed to make its Turbo sibling appear lethargic. That it happily provided a driving experience that was undiluted racer has only strengthened the GT2's case for a place within the Porsche annals as one of the greatest race and road cars ever to have been produced by the Stuttgart firm.

Today's 996-generation GT2 is essentially the same vehicle, but different in significant ways. Whereas the original GT2 was designed as a racetrack competitor first, road car second, the 996 car was put together purely for the road, albeit very much on a race-car theme. The current GT2 took elements of its contemporary four-wheel-drive twin-turbo 911 and punched through the established boundaries. The four-wheel-drive system was left on the shelf for a start, and the 3.6-litre water-cooled flat-six engine again went under the engineers' spanners for a few delicate tweaks.

The changes centred on air flow, boost pressure and a reprogramming of the engine management system. The result was a 10 per cent increase over the 911 Turbo in both peak power and torque, with 462bhp produced at 5700rpm and 457lb/ft of torque produced from 3500rpm. With a power-to-weight figure of 320bhp per tonne, the current GT2 will complete the 0–60mph sprint in 4.1 seconds and go on to reach a 195mph maximum speed. Sitting 20mm lower than the Turbo, the GT2 also features fully adjustable springs and dampers, all of which have been uprated, and five- (front) and four-point (rear) adjustable anti-roll bars. The car's ride height, camber and track are fully adjustable too.

Harnessing all this power is Porsche's revolutionary Ceramic Composite Brake system, which features a set of 350mm cross-drilled and ventilated ceramic brake discs weighing 50 per cent less than the steel items used on the Turbo. Composite brake pads are also used, and all discs are clamped by six- (front) and four-piston (rear) calipers. A set of 8J x 18in (front) and 12J x 18in (rear) alloy wheels adorn the GT2 and are wrapped in 235/40ZR18 and 315/30ZR18 rubber front to rear.

Developed from the 911 Turbo's body shell, the GT2 takes the 996 shape to its most extreme evolution yet. Both front and rear spoilers have been re-profiled following extensive trials in the wind tunnel, and the result is a host of scoops and ducts from nose to tail. Aerodynamically, the GT2 features a composite lower front spoiler to minimize underbody air flow, thus reducing front-end lift while increasing grip and directional stability at high speed. At the rear there are two aerodynamic aids: the first a discreet lip spoiler situated on the engine cover, the other a five-stage adjustable rear wing. In terms of functionality, the GT2's body alterations also include a number of fundamental scoops and ducts. At either end of the front bumper is a pair of inlets to channel cool air into those brakes, while a larger, more substantial duct feeds air into the front-mounted radiator before expelling it out and over the body, which again assists in reducing lift at high speed.

Internally, the GT2 is race ready. Beautifully sculptured Recaro seats hold you firmly in place, while a half roll cage sits proudly behind you. However, this is the twenty-first century, and Porsche decided that it could relax its stripped-out rules and has kitted out the 996 GT2 with central locking, electric windows, air conditioning and a CD radio. They don't make racing specials like they used to.

Actually, they do, because as anyone who has been fortunate enough to drive or be a

This page The stunning GT2, from the 996 generation, showing the luxurious electrically-equipped interior and the neat rear positioning of the powerfully updated flat-six engine. Is this the ultimate Porsche?

passenger in one will testify, the GT2 feels like no other road car. The punch of acceleration on offer from that flat-six motor is enough to make your eyes bleed. The speed with which the GT2 goes from 100mph to 150mph is, quite literally, unbelievable, but it's not nearly as impressive as the way in which it stops.

The GT2 has been criticized for its lack of involvement. Supposedly there is a certain something wanting in this model that means it falls short of being a great 911 in the same way as a 2.7 RS or 993 GT2. Whatever the purists' view, there is no denying that the 996 GT2 is one hell of a motor car, and one fantastic Porsche.

PORSCHE
Today

The global car market is a scary place for small independent sports car manufacturers. Ferrari is owned by Fiat, as is Maserati. Ford weigh in with Aston Martin and Jaguar, while VAG are at the controls of Lamborghini and Bugatti. And things seem to be going well for companies that have traditionally struggled to survive: Lamborghini has recently launched a Diablo replacement, Bugatti's £650,000 250mph Veyron should become a production reality, Aston's new Vanquish has just hit the streets to much acclaim, and Ferrari continues to produce stunning sports cars and Grand Prix victories. For the parent companies, these polished gems, dripping with history and exotic allure, provide that all-important sparkle, a little reflected glory for the parents' more mundane offerings to bathe in. But the last decade was one of solid financial growth and stability, and with the threat of a financial downturn looming large in the opening years of the twenty-first century and the prospect of empty order books for those in the supercar business, what will become of those great names should the bank balance turn from black to red? Would a giant such as Ford or VW really shed a tear if it was forced to 'dispose' of a loss-making financial dinosaur? Maybe, maybe not. For many, the red ink is more than compensated for by the glamour of the sports car market.

Porsche has found itself competing in an ever more ferocious struggle for market share, and against far bigger guns than used to be trained in its direction. Nevertheless, red ink is not something the Stuttgart concern is used to having to deal with in recent times. In 2001, Porsche's pre-tax returns on sales stood at 11.9 per cent, which made it the world's most profitable motor car manufacturer – a position made all the more impressive by the fact that it was forced to commit considerable development expenses to the Cayenne project. The company produced more cars than ever from its Zuffenhausen plant that year, proving that efficiency levels are ever improving. An all-new state-of-the-art production facility, built on a greenfield site near Leipzig, is also approaching fully operational status.

The brand-new Cayenne 4x4 cross-country vehicle is on the roads, the Carrera GT ultra car becoming production reality in the near future. With the revised 911 range incorporating several new variants, and an all-new Boxster due within the next couple of years, Porsche's future looks exceptionally bright. Its efficiency, output and profits have risen without the exclusivity of the brand ever being compromised.

Previous page Beauty, performance and practicality, the 2002 9114S shows how stylishly the Porsche equation continues to balance in the twenty-first century.

This page The 1993 concept model of the Porsche Boxster, with its sleek bodylines and stunning interior, immediately grabs the attention. The exterior was styled by two young Porsche designers and won great acclaim.

Opposite page The Boxster in road form: this is one of the original 1997 Boxster 2.5 models. Not quite as pretty as the concept model, mostly for reasons of practicality, it still sold well until retired in favour of a 2.7-litre version in 1999.

THE BOXSTER

When the Boxster concept first broke cover at the Detroit Motor Show in 1993, the jaws of onlookers dropped to the floor. The styling, by young Porsche designers Grant Larson and Stefan Stark, was fabulous, evoking memories of the 550 Spyder, of James Dean and of late 1950s cool. The interior, like the exterior, melded past, present and future with backlit dials, exposed gear linkage and tailored seats. Even the name was a modern interpretation of two classic Porsche trademarks: the 'Boxer' horizontally opposed power units and the 'Speedster' name first seen on the 356.

When it became a production reality in 1996, it didn't quite recreate the perfect synergy of retro detailing and state-of-the-art technology the show car had promised. The cost constraints of building a car to compete with offerings from BMW and Mercedes had taken some of the concept's visual flair away. Other problems were caused by practicality. The concept's curved doors didn't allow good enough access, while the low air intakes provided insufficient cooling for the engine and had to be replaced by the larger, higher items the car features today. Even the slender front wings had to be enlarged in order to house a radiator each. The finished product was a little slab-sided, the overhangs were a little larger, and the less kindly disposed claimed to have difficulty in ascertaining which way it was facing. The interior, too, was more sombrely conventional. There was, perhaps, an element of not wanting to overshadow the 911 with the flashy young upstart.

It is easy to overlook, now that Porsche is flourishing once more, the level of importance the company attached to the Boxster. Those aforementioned forays into the roadster market from BMW and Mercedes came at a time when Japanese interest had all but been withdrawn. A new, hugely profitable niche had

1997 Porsche Boxster (2.5)

Engine

Power unit: six-cylinder, horizontally opposed, water-cooled
Capacity: 2480cc
Location: mid-mounted
Valves: four valves per cylinder
Construction: aluminium alloy
Bore x stroke: 85.5mm x 72mm
Compression ratio: 11.0:1
Fuel system: Motronic
Power: 204bhp @ 6000rpm
Torque: 180lb/ft @ 4500rpm
Transmission: five-speed manual, rear-wheel drive

Suspension

Front: MacPherson struts, coil springs, anti-roll bar
Rear: MacPherson struts, multi-link, coil springs, anti-roll bar

Brakes

Front and rear: cross-drilled and ventilated discs, four-pot calipers, four-wheel ABS-5

Wheels

Front: Pressure-cast light alloys, 6J x 16in
Rear: Pressure-cast light alloys, 7J x 16in

Tyres

Front: 205/55 ZR16
Rear: 225/50 ZR16

Dimensions

Length: 4133mm
Wheelbase: 2400mm
Width: 1740mm
Weight: 1260kg

Performance

Maximum speed: 155mph
0–60mph: 7.4 seconds

opened up for 'premium brand', affordable sports cars. If Porsche was to buck the economic doldrums that had snared its single-model line-up, it had to take a share of the spoils. A new customer base was waiting, people who had grown up idolizing the 911 but for whom it was still beyond their means. The Boxster was a more readily available Porsche, but it was imperative that it be a Porsche: history had shown that a 'poor man's Porsche' would flop. There was no doubting that the Boxster was very much a Porsche to look at: lean, well proportioned and brimming with family heritage, it was modern and at the same time ageless. The proof of its quality, if it were needed, lies in the fact that Porsche has barely changed it since its debut. They got things pretty much spot-on first time round.

Porsche had instantly realized that people would want more from this entry-level Porsche. A sport package was soon on offer, upping wheel size to 17in and offering stiffer tuned suspension. A hard top was also an option (and a popular one, in the UK at least), which added to the car's practicality and made the looks a little more 911-like.

1999 was the year that really brought the Boxster range to life. The standard 2.5 was ditched in favour of a 220bhp, 2.7-litre version which also boasted an extra 12lb/ft of torque. The chassis could still cope easily with the extra urge, and the 2.7 seemed a far better proposition, much quicker in terms of day-to-day driving than was suggested by a 0–60mph time just four-tenths of a second quicker than its predecessor. The other

newcomer in 1999, and the one to excite the enthusiasts, was the Boxster S. There wasn't much to differentiate the S from the 2.7, only 17in wheels and red brake calipers, a twin exit tail pipe, the odd subtle graphic and some titanium-effect trim. Truth was, with a 3.2-litre engine and 246bhp, it was not only the finest Boxster in the range, it was also one of the most accomplished sports cars on the planet.

The Boxster was the perfect response to the recession-hit 1990s, opening up the Porsche brand to a whole new marketplace without sacrificing the engineering integrity and driving dynamics for which the marque was revered. It was Porsche's first new sports car in very nearly 23 years. The Boxster had to succeed; it had to outhandle and outperform BMW's Z3 and Mercedes's SLK, and it had to woo buyers back to Porsche. It succeeded in every area, with devastating conviction. Its striking headlamp assemblies have now become the 'face' of the entire Porsche model line-up, including the upcoming Cayenne sporting off-roader. Its use of water-cooled engines has similarly been adopted in the 911. It is revered by the motoring enthusiast for its impeccable balance, unimpeachable handling and fabulous engine. Residual values remain absolutely rock-solid, and few of its rivals can compare as an ownership experience.

Above *The mechanical construct of the Boxster, showing the low-mounted engine.*

Opposite page *Cutaway view of the entry-level Boxster 2.5.*

Porsche is continuing to tweak and evolve the Boxster to make it ever more appealing, and it is due for a comprehensive makeover towards the end of 2002. More upmarket trim and switchgear will lift the cabin ambience and counter criticisms that the Boxster's interior lacks sparkle, and it is also rumoured that the Boxster S will gain access to a version of the 3.4-litre flat-six used originally in the early 996. With close to 300bhp, it should make the S an even more fearsome performer, with the wherewithal to take on BMW's all-new Z3 M Roadster and a new V6-engined Audi TT. Porsche owes a lot to the Boxster's sales success, but then again that success would never have occurred had Porsche not made its new baby such an appealing and prodigiously talented piece of kit.

MODEL IN FOCUS: BOXSTER S

When the Boxster S hit the streets in 1999 with its 246bhp 3.2-litre version of the water-cooled flat-six, it answered the critics and the enthusiasts who had bemoaned the fact that the Boxster's pin-sharp chassis was capable of handling so much more performance. For the 2002 model year, the Boxster gains another six horsepower, which will translate into a 0–60mph time of less than six seconds and a top speed on the other side of 160mph. The 'S' may as well stand for 'superior', because that is what Porsche intended the car to be, in every department, to the standard Boxster: even faster, even more powerful, even safer.

Whereas there is no mistaking a standard 911 Carrera for a GT2, the visual distinctions between the standard Boxster and the 'S' are a little more subtle. The 'S' gets seventeen-inch alloy wheels with a unique design as standard. Look closer, and you'll notice the brake calipers

Below and opposite page The 1999 Boxster S was a far superior model to the original 2.5, although visually there were few differences apart from the attractive silver dials and the optional in-car entertainment systems.

are painted red. Those aren't standard-issue Boxster anchors, either. The seventeen-inch wheels have been fitted to allow Porsche's engineers to sneak in the 318mm discs from the 996 Carrera behind them, cross-drilled for further efficacy. The rears are up to 299mm in diameter with four-piston calipers all round. These formidable stoppers are more than a match for the extra power the 'S' has under the engine bay, especially with their all-new dedicated cooling system, which according to Porsche's pre-launch publicity 'increases the durability of the brakes, even under the heaviest use'. It may be in case you're tempted to test this that they've added a full-spec safety kit to the 'S': standard equipment includes the Porsche Side Impact Protection system (POSIP), although the Porsche Stability Management system (PSM) remains an option. They're obviously aware how desirable it is too: an alarm system with interior surveillance comes as standard, so if it isn't yours don't get too close.

If you're still unconvinced it's an 'S' and are only able to admire from outside, look out for the 'Boxster S' model designation on the door strips either side. You may also notice the extra titanium-coloured air scoop at the front of the 'S', but in fairness you're more likely to spot the subtle badging at the rear, or perhaps the twin central tail pipes. If you're lucky enough to have found an 'S' parked next to a standard Boxster, you may notice that while the 'S' is a hand's width longer, its wheelbase is marginally shorter. If good fortune should place you inside, the eagle-eyed may espy the silver-grey dial faces and their aluminium-look bezels, part of a general style makeover by the designers, or the additional sixth gear, added by the Stuttgart factory to ease gear changing in all situations. But if you're already inside, the easiest way to tell is to fire it up. If you dare.

2002 Porsche Boxster S

Engine
Power unit: six-cylinder, horizontally opposed, water-cooled
Capacity: 3596cc
Location: mid-mounted
Valves: four valves per cylinder
Construction: aluminium alloy
Bore x stroke: 85.5mm x 72mm
Compression ratio: 11.3:1
Fuel system: Motronic
Power: 320bhp @ 6800rpm
Torque: 273lb/ft @ 4250rpm
Transmission six-speed manual, four-wheel drive (optional Tiptronic S)

Suspension
Front: MacPherson struts, coil springs, anti-roll bar
Rear: MacPherson struts, multi-link, coil springs, anti-roll bar

Brakes
Front and rear: cross-drilled and ventilated discs, four-pot monobloc calipers, ABS, ASR, ABD

Wheels
Front: Pressure-cast light alloys, 7J x 17in
Rear: Pressure-cast light alloys, 9J x 17in

Tyres
Front: 205/50 ZR17
Rear: 255/40 ZR17

Dimensions
Length: 4430mm
Wheelbase: 2350mm
Width: 1770mm
Weight: 1540kg

Performance
Maximum speed: 174mph
0–60mph: 5.7 seconds

Above The 996 evolution of the 911 Carrera offered a new aerodynamic shape and 3.4-litre water-cooled engine, which proved a winning combination despite early unpopularity among the Porsche cognoscenti.

Below The water-cooled engine of the 996, with its Motronic EMS and catalytic converter.

THE 996

In 1997, Porsche sent 911 purists everywhere into shock with the launch of the 996 incarnation of its stalwart 911 model. This represented the biggest evolutionary step forward since the 911's launch, both in terms of visual alteration and technical change. Inevitably with a vehicle that has such a cult following, some people were unhappy with the new Porsche flagship, though time, as it will, proved some of them very wrong indeed. Porsche knew it had to give the 911 the right equipment to keep it competitive well into the third millennium, and that would mean serious changes. Unbeknown to most people, the Boxster had been more than just a new model; it had been a testbed for new ideas, radical new technologies that would be showcased on the new 911.

There were several areas Porsche had to address and seriously improve in the 911. The competition was constantly upping its game, and Porsche had to follow suit in order to keep the 911 legend alive. Firstly, the air-cooled flat-six needed attention, though the designation had to remain the same. Some engines are simply synonymous with certain cars: think Ford Mustang, think V8; think BMW M3, think straight-six; think Lamborghini Diablo – well, anything less than a V12 would be scandalous! So Porsche persisted with the Boxster arrangement, claiming it was ideal because of its compact dimensions and short, stiff crank facilitating high engine speeds. In the 996, though, it would be water-cooled for the first time. Packing 3.4 litres, 300bhp and a rippling 258lb/ft of torque, it might not have had the 993's distinctive air-cooled beat, but it compensated for it with improved thermal stability and increased potency – and few could dispute the proposition that it is still one of the most characterful engine notes around. Plus, with its advanced Motronic ME 7.2 engine management system teamed with the latest catalyst technology, it is clean enough to comply with the most stringent emissions regulations. Fortunately, the engine remains located behind the rear axle, maintaining the traditional 911 theme.

With the engine covered, attention was turned to the bodywork. The brief wasn't easy: retain the evocative 911 silhouette but improve aerodynamics, occupant accommodation and safety, and luggage space. No problem. The 996 has a slippery, lozenge-like shape which lowers the drag coefficient from the 993's 0.34 to just 0.3, despite a larger frontal area. Also, lifting forces on the front and rear axles were seriously reduced to afford the car superb stability at high speeds. Some people aimed criticisms at the shape, claiming that the new car had lost the muscular haunches of the 993. Indeed, the 993 remains the ultimate 911 for many, but Porsche knew it had to endow the 996 with superior aerodynamics, and the pay-off of the wider body was also felt inside. All but the very tallest can get comfortable in the cabin of the 996, with its improved elbow room and plenty of travel fore and aft in the front seats. With leather, electric seats and air conditioning, there are plenty of toys and luxuries as well. Luggage space was also important, considering the 911's reputation as a supreme Grand Tourer and genuinely practical

Above *The 996 being road-tested in the USA.*

Below *The 911 Carrera of 1997. The distinctive shape of the 996 echoed Porsche's past while remaining totally up to date*

Porsche 911 (996) 3.4 Carrera 2

Engine
Power unit: six-cylinder, air-cooled
Capacity: 3387cc
Location: rear
Valves: four per cylinder
Construction: Aluminium
Bore x stroke: 96mm x 78mm
Compression ratio: 11.3:1
Fuel system: Sequential multi-point fuel injection with DME Engine management
Power: 300bhp @ 6800rpm
Torque: 258lb/ft @ 4600rpm
Transmission: six-speed manual; five-speed Tiptronic S

Suspension
Front: independent MacPherson struts with coil springs, lower wishbones, anti-roll bar
Rear: independent semi-trailing arms, transverse torsion bars, telescopic dampers, anti-roll bar

Brakes
Front: 305mm ventilated discs, ABS
Rear: 300mm ventilated discs, ABS

Wheels
Front: 7J x 17in
Rear: 9J x 17in

Tyres
Front: 205/50 ZR17
Rear: 225/40 ZR17

Dimensions
Length: 4430mm
Wheelbase: 2350mm
Width: 1765mm
Weight: 1320kg

Performance
Maximum speed: 175mph; 171mph with Tiptronic S
0–60mph: 5.2 seconds; 6 seconds with Tiptronic S

everyday supercar. The front luggage compartment offered 130 litres of stowage, with another 200 litres available in the rear of the passenger cell, with the back seats tilted down.

So it looks good, slices through the air better than ever, offers improved accommodation for passengers and luggage, and has more power. But without raising the 993's ability on the roads, the 996 adds nothing to the 911 legend. Fortunately, it delivers in spades. From the moment you slot the rifle-bolt precise gearshift into the first of its six forward ratios (a five-speed Tiptronic option was also available from launch), it feels a more sophisticated experience than its predecessors. Thrust from the 3.4-litre unit is strong and linear, with a rich, subtle soundtrack that really comes alive towards the top of the rev range. Each new gear plants the engine right back into its sweet spot, and as the 996 speeds into three figures it remains stable, controlled and unintimidating.

You never forget the 996 is rear-engined. Every time you turn in with the fabulously uncorrupted steering, the car seems to pivot from a point over your shoulder and you zero in on the apex. The rear suspension utilizes five control arms on each wheel, allowing alteration in their toe-in position. On the road, this translates to gentle understeer, letting the driver know that the limits of adhesion are being approached. Four-pot brake calipers using technology from the Le Mans 24-Hour cars ensure fade-free response even after prolonged fast driving, while added security comes in the form of optional Porsche Stability Management (PSM) traction control.

It wasn't until 1998, however, that the hardcore 911 fans really had a 996 to call their own. Tied inevitably to motorsport involvement, the limited-production, stripped-out, 360bhp aero-kitted GT3 was an

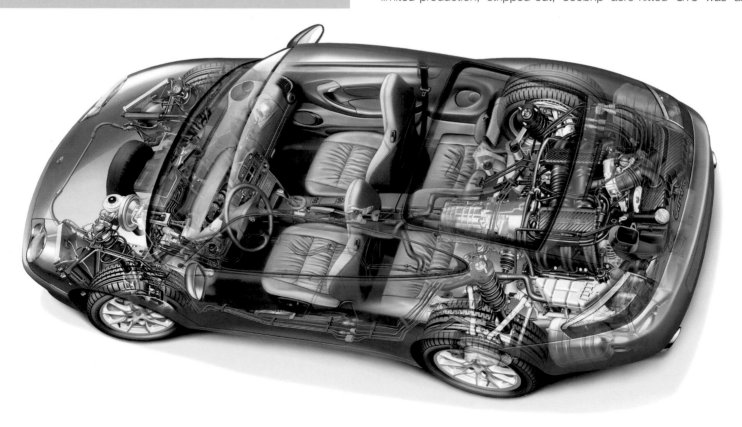

This page and opposite *The 2001 Porsche Carrera 4S continues the 996 line into the twenty-first century with sleek looks, proven turbo power and astonishing straight-line performance.*

This page A new face for a new millennium. The 2000 911 Turbo was a winner with its stunning looks and low ground clearance, and towering performance.

instant classic. It was capable of 0–60mph in just 4.8 seconds and a 187mph maximum speed. In the hands of twice world rally champion Walter Röhrl, it smashed the benchmark eight-minute time at the Nürburgring by four seconds. Its incredible performance was not only down to the increased engine performance. The brakes were beefed up to 330mm in diameter, tucked behind lightweight 18in wheels, and suspension was revised, reinforced and lowered by a hefty 30mm, a drop made to seem even more impressive by the inclusion of a more aggressive front end and side skirts, which were teamed to an imposing rear wing to leave onlookers in no doubt of this vehicle's performance credentials. Adjustable anti-roll bars were fitted, and the provision for racing springs, along with increased geometry adjustments, allowed quick and complete tailoring for track use. The interior did away with rear seats to pare away precious kilograms, while the fronts were lightweight and extremely supportive on road and track. The car could also be ordered with a roll cage for superior rigidity.

The last year of the second millennium could have been a sad one for Porsche enthusiasts as the GT3 became defunct. Fortunately, Stuttgart softened the blow by diverting our attention

Left *Porsche finally delivered up a cabriolet version of its 996-generation 911 in 2000. Its electrically-operated hood and a wide range of optional luxuries made it a firm favourite.*

Below *The 2002 911 Carrera Cabriolet.*

with the wild 414bhp four-wheel-drive 996 Turbo. The twin-turbocharged 3.6-litre engine might have been fundamentally the same as its air-cooled predecessor, but the introduction of water-cooling along with VarioCam Plus (which allowed the engine management to adjust valve-lift to suit driving conditions) helped liberate a whopping 413lb/ft of torque from as little as 2700rpm. With the Turbo's scintillating traction from its four-wheel-drive system, it launched past 60mph in a shade over four seconds on its way to 190mph. No longer was the 911 Turbo deserving of the 'scary' tag, for the 996 Turbo was easy to drive at astonishing pace. It combined mind-blowing straight-line shove with the sort of cornering grip few cars could

match. Some purists bemoaned the fact that it lacked the involvement and ultimate thrill of the 993 Turbo, but the 996 was, and is, the ultimate all-weather supercar.

For 2001, the 996 range received a number of revisions and upgrades. The Carrera models had capacity increased to 3596cc, with a corresponding power hike to 320bhp. The Turbo donated not only its headlights to the rest of the range but also its trip computer. Purists might want to make sure there's a seat handy, because the 911 is now available with a glovebox and a cup holder! Stuttgart has made a couple of concessions to the old guard, though: the latest 911s have been given back that familiar air-cooled bass note, redressing complaints that the newer models sounded flat and uninspiring.

With the glass-roofed Targa, cabriolet and the turbo-bodied Carrera 4S available, as well as the GT2 and Turbo models, there is great depth to the 911 range. With enthusiasm for it seemingly as strong as ever, it is hard to imagine Porsche without its core car. It's been with us for nearly 40 years already, and the 996 has set it along the road to 40 more.

Above and opposite page The four-wheel-drive Carrera 4S for the 2002 model year offers impressive performance with searing 5.1-second 0–60 acceleration and a top speed of 177mph.

THE CAYENNE

Late 2002 will see the launch of a third model in the Porsche range. The Cayenne, described by Porsche as a 'cross-country car', is set to net the company a fair chunk of the lucrative Sport Utility Vehicle (SUV) marketplace, but it will face stiff and well-established opposition from Lexus, Mercedes and BMW. The all-new Range Rover has also been launched, featuring state-of-the-art cabin design and the kind of off-road capabilities that leave the competition reeling. Porsche is, of course, aiming for a more sporting and dynamic interpretation, but that doesn't mean it will have an easy time of it.

The class-leading BMW X5 will surely be the Cayenne's sternest test. The X5 has already been around for a couple of years now, and has established a huge following around the world. Such has been its impact that it is almost single-handedly responsible for transforming America into a marketplace to match (and soon eclipse) Germany. Praised for its subtle and car-like road manners, serious performance and subtle style, the X5 is not only talented, it is unmistakably a BMW.

Whether the Cayenne has been able to pull off the same trick so convincingly is a matter for some conjecture. The car features a typical Porsche nose, with 911-style headlamps and large air scoops, but the rear has provided a new challenge for the designers in Stuttgart. No Porsche has ever had to afford five-door practicality and accommodation for five adults and their luggage and associated paraphernalia. Early reactions to official pictures at the 2002 Geneva Motor Show were mixed. The car is definitely full of Porsche DNA, but whether or not it works as a cohesive whole is difficult to assess. Several reporters described it as 'the Porker' for its chunky, unusual-for-Porsche shape. But it has already sold out in pre-order in the UK for some 25,000 units, so the dedicated Porsche enthusiast is obviously keen to try it out.

Moreover, BMW has just raised the performance stakes, aiming straight for the Cayenne's jugular with the new X5 4.6is. Boasting

Porsche Cayenne Turbo 'S'

Engine
Power unit: eight cylinders in vee
Capacity: 4587cc
Location: front
Valves: four per cylinder
Construction: unknown
Bore x stroke: unknown
Compression ratio: unknown
Fuel system: unknown
Power: 450bhp @ unknown rpm
Torque: 457lb/ft @ unknown rpm
Transmission: six-speed Tiptronic S with high and low ratios

Suspension
Front and rear: independent, air springs, height adjustable

Brakes
Front and rear: ventilated discs, six-piston calipers, four-channel ABS

Wheels
Front: 7J x 17in
Rear: 9J x 17in

Tyres
Front: 205/50 ZR17
Rear: 225/40 ZR17

Dimensions
Length: 4782mm
Wheelbase: 2855mm
Width: 1928mm
Weight: unknown

Performance
Maximum speed: 165mph
0–60mph: 5.6 seconds

Right *A new direction for 2002: the Cayenne 4x4 Turbo. Despite its hefty appearance, it is has quite stunning performance courtesy of its turbo V8 engine.*

Bottom *The slightly more sedate Cayenne S, which aims to put Porsche squarely into the family-car market.*

almost 350bhp from its V8 powerplant, the 4.6is is capable of sprinting to 60mph in just six and a half seconds on the way to almost 150mph. That's quick enough to scare a Boxster, and will mean the Cayenne needs serious performance in order to compete. Fortunately, it seems Porsche won't be easily outdone, and industry rumours claim that the turbocharged V8 version is quicker around a lap of the infamous Nürburgring's northern loop than a Boxster S!

There will be two versions of an all-new 32-valve 4.5-litre V8 power unit on offer at the Cayenne's launch. The normally aspirated 'S' version will give 340bhp, while the Turbo will offer a mighty 450bhp. Additional front air inlets, power domes on the hood, and four exhaust tailpipes help distinguish the Cayenne Turbo from the Cayenne S. A 3.2-litre V6 with around 240bhp will join the range as an entry-level offering later on, and there are plans for a V8 diesel lump (yes, really, a Porsche diesel!) to join the ranks in a couple of years' time.

Official performance figures are only provisional at this time, but early estimates for the V8 S talk of a 0–60mph time in the region of seven seconds and the ability to charge on to 150mph. The Turbo, meanwhile, is set to hit sixty in well under six seconds flat on the way to 165mph – incredible for a jacked-up two-tonne-plus vehicle, the kind of figures you'd expect to be associated with a 911, not an off-roader.

The Cayenne – built at a newly constructed factory in Leipzig but designed, of course, in Stuttgart – will feature an all-new six-speed Tiptronic S gearbox, exclusive to both models. The transmission features both low and high ratios and is mated to the four-wheel-drive system via a central differential capable of juggling drive fore and aft, depending on requirements. The front and rear differentials will also be lockable for extra off-road ability. PSM traction control will also be standard. The Cayenne will use advanced air springs too, developed jointly with VW, featuring full height adjustability, with large discs and six-pot calipers doing the braking. The Turbo will be distinguished by subtle bonnet bulges and quad tail pipes.

Porsche is obviously concerned that people take its third model seriously, having launched the Cayenne publicity campaign several months before the model is due to hit the streets. The adverts feature a shot of a fully liveried 959

thundering across the most rugged of landscapes on its way to the 1985 Paris–Dakar victory; the legend reads: 'Only a Porsche has a bloodline like this.' Stirring stuff, but the 959 was far from an unqualified success. One belated Paris–Dakar victory and the fact that each road car cost the factory twice as much as its price tag saw Porsche's Group B experiment cut short. Nevertheless, there's no doubting Porsche's commitment to making the Cayenne a success. Only time will tell the story. Traditionally, only Porsche's core models have truly succeeded, but the triumph of the Boxster proved that this needn't be the case. Today's buyers want exclusivity, they want to stand out from the crowd, and the brand they buy speaks for them. Here Porsche has tremendous clout: few brands have the undiluted impact of the Porsche name. Plus, there has never been a Porsche aimed so squarely at the affluent family man. Despite two-plus-two pretensions, no Porsche has ever provided comfortable or usable rear passenger space, or the associated luggage stowage. In this regard, the Cayenne dips its toe into a potentially huge new marketplace. Early signs for the Cayenne's future are good, Porsche dealers worldwide reporting massive interest in the sports off-roader despite a noteable lack of technical information emerging from the factory to public gaze, and the company is contemplating upping its sales targets, which already stand at an estimated 25,000 units per annum and represent an increase in sales volume of almost 50 per cent.

Above The front styling of the Cayenne Turbo has drawn unwelcome comparisons with less esteemed marques, but it shows early promise as a new venture.

THE CARRERA GT

Porsche caused quite a stir at the Paris Motor Show in 2000 when they unveiled a radical new supercar concept: the Carrera GT. The fabulously exotic-looking open-top two-seater showcased a 5.5-litre mid-mounted V10 engine with an alleged power output of 558bhp and 443lb/ft of torque. Few people at the time thought it would become a production reality, but since then the supercar landscape has changed dramatically and Porsche are suddenly in

2002 Porsche Carrera GT

Engine

Power unit: 68° V10, air-cooled
Capacity: 5500cc
Location: mid-mounted
Valves: four valves per cylinder
Construction: all light alloy
Bore x stroke: unknown
Compression ratio: unknown
Fuel system: unknown
Power: 558bhp
Torque: 443lb/ft
Transmission: six-speed manual, rear-wheel drive

Suspension

General: anti-roll bar, spring/damper unit operated by push rods
Front: double-wishbone axle, power-assisted rack and pinion
Rear: double wishbone

Brakes

General: twin circuit ABS, Porsche Ceramic Composite brake discs
Front: 380mm discs, eight-piston aluminium calipers
Rear: 380mm discs, four-piston aluminium calipers

Wheels

Front and rear: forged light alloys

Tyres

Front: 265/30 R19
Rear: 335/30 R20

Dimensions

Length: 4556mm
Wheelbase: 2700mm
Width: 1915mm (excluding mirrors)
Weight: 1250kg

Performance

Maximum speed: over 206mph
0–60mph: under four seconds

need of a new über-model to compete in the supercar stratosphere. With positive feedback from potential customers, Porsche has decided that there is a market for the Carrera GT, and at the Detroit Motor Show in January 2002 it was announced that the car would go into a limited production of 1,000 models and go on sale late in 2003 priced at a cool £250,000.

Although the show car was 'only' a roadster, the road car will have, in the words of the Porsche president, a 'good-looking roof mechanism'. Other changes to the production model will be different door handles and revised headlamp assemblies, and there will also be a revamped automatically raising rear wing, but the technical specification should remain very close to that of the concept.

Racing is at the very heart of the Carrera GT's design. The imposing front air scoop not only provides airflow to the radiator, but also to the massive 380mm front brake discs, with ducts at the rear providing an outlet for the dissipated heat. Clamped by eight-piston calipers, the brakes will provide mind-blowing retardation. The air scoops on the rear of the flanks also provide cooling air to the rear brakes, but their chief task is to aid engine cooling – a vital aspect of the design with such an extreme powerplant. The rear wing is designed to lift at speeds above 75mph to provide negative lift, while a diffuser-shaped underbody provides additional downforce on the rear axle.

The all-alloy engine is exceptionally light, weighing in at just 165kg. It replaces traditional cylinder linings with a low-friction Nikasil surface, which allows the engine to be shortened. The pistons themselves are forged aluminium, while the con-rods are constructed from super-strong titanium. The engine also utilizes racer-style dry-sump lubrication. The results are quoted as being 'at least' 558bhp, with a redline above 8000rpm. The powerplant's lightweight, high-tech specification is mirrored by the use of a carbon-fibre monocoque and aluminium frame. Again using racing car know-how, the drive train and suspension are incorporated, with the spring struts for the rear axle pivoting on the six-speed gearbox. The suspension itself will be fully adjustable, allowing the driver to tailor the perfect handling set-up. Despite these extraordinarily advanced engineering measures, Porsche have decided not to exploit quite such extreme weight-savings in the cockpit, assuming that anybody wishing to spend a quarter of a million pounds on their car deserves leather upholstery, air conditioning and electric windows. That isn't to say the driving environment won't be a match for the twenty-first-century technology, however. The Carrera GT will feature a full colour monitor in place of the traditional instrument cluster which will allow the driver to monitor all the car's vital statistics. There will be a number of different interface 'levels', with one aimed at road use and a different set of parameters for racetrack use. The centre console is sharply angled up towards the dashboard with the gear lever mounted high, barely a hand's width from the steering wheel. The design is also said to increase the car's torsional rigidity. Given the incredible levels of cornering grip the Carrera GT will be capable of delivering, the seats will also feature retractable leg and knee supports to aid driver comfort. A hint of practicality is suggested by the provision of forward-mounted luggage space.

Early indications show that the Carrera GT's performance will be utterly shattering, with the awesome McLaren F1 being used as a benchmark. Expect 0–60mph to be obliterated in under four seconds, 125mph to pass in under ten seconds, and a top speed well in excess of 200mph. And with Mercedes on the cusp of launching its own SLR supercar, developed in

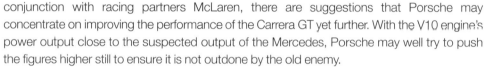

conjunction with racing partners McLaren, there are suggestions that Porsche may concentrate on improving the performance of the Carrera GT yet further. With the V10 engine's power output close to the suspected output of the Mercedes, Porsche may well try to push the figures higher still to ensure it is not outdone by the old enemy.

When the Carrera GT finally hits the streets, it will have its work cut out to be considered the ultimate, but things are looking good. The styling is instantly recognizable – this car could only be a Porsche. Technologically it is more akin to a Formula One car than a traditional road car, and it packs enough of that ground-breaking technology to keep Porsche ahead of the game. Needless to say, the motoring fraternity are bristling with anticipation at the prospect of Porsche's latest offering.

Above *The Carrera GT concept model, as seen at the Paris Motor Show in 2000 – 100 years since Ferdinand Porsche's first car was demonstrated at the Paris Expo. Due to outclass the McLaren F1 in performance and style, this piece of motoring exotica will hit the streets in 2003 in a strictly limited edition of 1000 cars.*

THE FUTURE

CEO and president of Porsche Dr Wendelin Wiedeking, who took up his current position back in 1992, has recently had his contract extended to 2007. This kind of stability has been crucial to Porsche's success. Wiedeking is a man who understands that Porsche needs to grow, though not without restraint. It must grow to meet new challenges, to improve efficiency and to exploit new opportunities, but it must not grow too fast. Porsche is proof that David can succeed in a world of Goliaths, but the company knows it must continue to prove itself on road and track again and again.

With the company's model range just about to double – an expansion which includes a foray into an alien marketplace with the Cayenne – and an all-new production facility about to go operational, some may fear that Porsche has bitten off too much too quickly. In truth, it has had no choice. The landscape of its traditional marketplace has altered with alarming rapidity in recent years, with a multitude of major manufacturers now encroaching upon Porsche territory. Porsche now needs to reassert itself on the world stage. The Boxster and 911 remain the cornerstones, but with the Cayenne and the stupendous Carrera GT, Porsche has ideal weapons with which to reclaim the headlines. To quote Dr Wiedeking himself, 'The future does not belong only to those who are big, but also to those who are proficient. The future belongs to Porsche.'

chapter
nine

The
Motorsport
Models

'Racing improves the breed' was one of Professor Porsche's most strongly held beliefs, and from the very first model produced in the wake of World War II, Porsche has raced the cars it sells. It has used tracks around the world to test, develop, and innovate, and none of its road cars has been built without benefiting from the lessons learned in competition. Indeed, whereas other automotive companies funded their racing programmes with the profits from their road car businesses, Ferdinand and Ferry Porsche used track success to build a reputation for their road cars, viewing competition as the perfect means of promoting their products. This has remained Porsche policy to date.

This book would not be complete without a review of the German giant's glittering racing heritage. In the next chapter we look at some of the famous, and not so famous, names that helped pilot Porsche to its many victories, and at some of the events it made its own. But let us look first at some of the cars that created the legend.

1947 CISITALIA GP PROJECT

Tazio Nuvolari, one of the finest drivers in motor racing history, a Formula 1 legend of Michael Schumacher's stature, was faced with a dilemma immediately after World War II. His former team manager during his Alfa Romeo days, Enzo Ferrari, had yet to get his car-building enterprise up and running (Ferrari didn't begin Grand Prix racing proper until 1948), leaving Nuvolari to choose between an aging Maserati and an uncompetitive Fiat-based Cisitalia. At the helm of Cisitalia was a prominent Torinese industrialist, Signor Piero Dusio, who was desperate to break through to the top ranks of Formula 1 and benefit from the exposure such a stage offered. He needed a top design team, and found one at Gmünd.

The initial contact came when Nuvolari visited Carlo Abarth, whom Ferry Porsche had asked to be an agent for his company (the Italian-based Austrian ex-pat had far freer movement than the Gmünd concern enjoyed). After a number of meetings, Porsche was

Previous page Some of Porsche's greatest motorsport models from the past 50 years.

This page and opposite The 1947 Cisitalia Type 360, a revolutionary design by Ferry Porsche that sadly never made it to the racetrack for financial reasons. Note particularly its mid-mounted engine and the fuel tanks to each side.

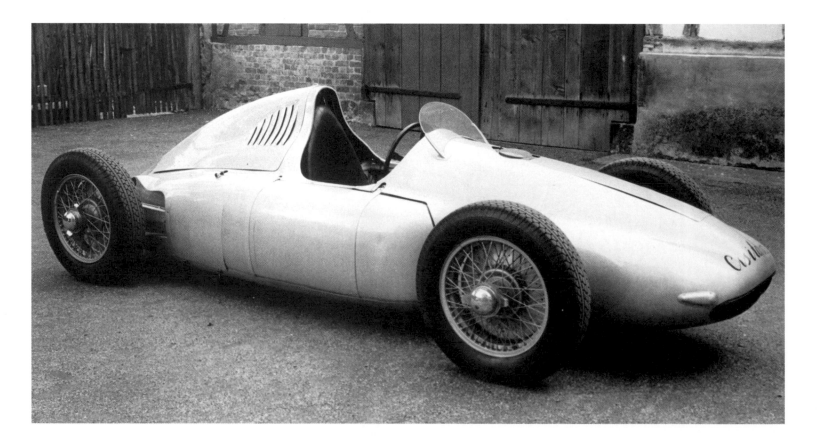

contracted in early 1947 to build four projects for Dusio. One of these was the Type 360 Grand Prix car. Its specification, even today, is impressive. Its tubular spaceframe chassis was the first of its kind and featured pannier-style fuel tanks running either side of the driver's seat. A relatively long wheelbase allowed the entire drive train, including the gearbox and clutch, to be located inside the rear axle, and the sleek lines were reminiscent of the all-conquering Auto Unions, although smaller in size.

The powerplant was incredible. It was a dual-compressor 1493cc water-cooled flat-twelve boxer, with quad overhead camshafts and twin superchargers, and was mounted in the centre of the chassis – a move that wouldn't be used in Formula 1 until John Cooper adopted it in 1950 but continues to this day. The only time it was tested it yielded an output of 385bhp at 10,600rpm and a top speed of 186mph – pretty impressive, but a potential figure of 450bhp was also mooted. Even more impressive was the fact that the five-speed gearbox was linked to a differential to allow the driver to switch between two- and four-wheel drive with individual drive activation of the front wheels.

Sadly, despite being shown to the public in 1949, the Type 360 was never raced. The relationship between Dusio and Porsche had cooled and the former was in dire financial trouble, leading to the end of the project shortly before his business collapsed. There's no doubt, though, that with its revolutionary technology and the genius of Tazio Nuvolari at the wheel, this first Porsche racing car venture could have made a huge splash in the Formula 1 arena. Designed and built in a ramshackle old sawmill, it was an effort of huge moment for the company, especially as much of it was accomplished before Porsche Senior was released from prison after the war. He was impressed by what had been done in his absence. A new era was dawning.

Above *The 1954 550 Spyder, in race trim as it appeared in the Carrera Panamericana of that year, where it was piloted to class victory by Hans Herrmann.*

Bottom right *The 500A RS of 1956. A similar car to that pictured won the Targa Florio with Maglioli and von Hanstein at the wheel and took a class win at Le Mans.*

THE 550

Porsche had been involved in motor racing from the word go, the 356 Gmünd prototype taking class honours in a road race in Innsbruck as early as 1948, and in 1951 Porsche made its debut at Le Mans with a 356 piloted by Auguste Veuillet and Edmond Mouche in the 1100cc class. Veuillet and Mouche won the class easily, and recorded a creditable twentieth place overall. It was less than a year later that work began on transforming the 356 into a 'proper' racing car. The company knew that there were risks involved: Porsche was still a small and therefore delicately poised company with only one model and nothing to fall back on. Fortunately, Ferry Porsche realized that the gains in terms of building a reputation for performance and advanced engineering were worth those risks. Since then, Porsche has never shied away from proving itself in competition.

The 550 was Porsche's first proper racing sports car. It was based heavily on the 356, in particular the mid-engined, open-topped 356 'special' built by German VW dealer and motorsport fanatic Walter Glöckler. With a simple, lightweight, ladder-frame chassis, a 1500cc flat-four and aerodynamic bodywork built by Wiedenhausen in Frankfurt, the first factory 550s appeared in 1953. Fuhrmann-engined, with a 1.5-litre four-cylinder unit, four gear-driven overhead camshafts and producing 100+ bhp on alcohol fuel, the 550 recorded a victory in its maiden race at the Nürburgring and was immediately entered for Le Mans. It ran in coupé guise for better aerodynamic performance on La Sarthe's long straights, while the engine power dropped to around 80bhp on petrol for better reliability. It was still, however, capable of topping 125mph on the Mulsanne, and went on to win the 1500cc category.

So promising was the 550's performance in its early runs under Richard von Frankenburg and others that the car was dubbed the 'shark in the pool of perch', referring to its outstanding achievements in major races against models with far more horsepower. By 1954, the 550 Spyder proper was on the scene, with over 110bhp, and the success continued. 550s won both 1500cc and 1100cc classes at Le Mans that year, but the most crucial victory was in a support race for the Grand Prix at the Nürburgring: Porsche 550s dominated, filling the first four places and attracting a lot of publicity for the company. As a result, more private customers began to place orders. The following year, 1955, Le Mans was overshadowed by a tragic accident which killed Mercedes driver Pierre Levegh and some 85 spectators, but a Porsche 550 finished fourth overall, first in class, and topped 140mph on the Mulsanne straight.

This page *These further images of the 1956 550A show its redesigned rear end, which improved the car's aerodynamics and housed the modified suspension, and the massive grilles that helped cool the 130bhp rear-mounted engine.*

Major progress came in 1956 with the revised 550A RS (RennSport). The 'A' had a lighter spaceframe chassis and modified rear suspension. Power was increased to 130bhp and a five-speed gearbox was utilized. It was with this car that Porsche aimed to claim a huge prize: the Targa Florio. This ultra-tough Sicilian road race, first run in 1906, was a fearsome test of man and machine, but the 550, in the hands of Huschke von Hanstein and Umberto Maglioli, took victory first time out – the first of a record-breaking eleven outright Targa Florio wins for the marque.

THE 718: RSK, RS60 AND THE BERGSPYDER

The 718 RSK was a logical evolution of the 550A, again designed for racing (the 'K' referred to the layout of the torsion bar and suspension ball-joints). It used the same 1500cc mid-mounted engine as its predecessor, but the innovative front suspension allowed a lower, more slippery body. Porsche further enhanced the RSK's wind-cheating ability by fairing-in the headlamps.

Early tests showed the RSK had great grip and potential, and from the start it could reach 155 mph on the track, but its torsion-bar rear suspension made it tricky to recover once traction had been breached. Revisions were soon put in place, and by 1958 it was truly competitive, taking third at Sebring on its first outing and second in the Targa Florio, ahead in each case of many more established race cars, including a number of 550 and 356 entrants. RSKs were third and fourth overall at Le Mans and dominated the 2-litre class.

The RSK was constantly evolving. In 1959, an increase in engine size from 1.5 to 1.6 litres produced an increased bhp of 148 – and the Targa Florio win, where the 718 headed a top four that was all Porsche (the others being a 550 RS and two 356A Carreras). The same year at Sebring five RSKs finished in the top ten, from several of the independent sportscar teams now thoroughly impressed with the little 718. It was a feat to be repeated at Buenos Aires in 1960, following a further redesign that changed the rear suspension to a double-wishbone and coil spring formation. After this a new variation on the 718 theme, the RS60, took over the World Sports Car events.

The RS60 was basically a Formula 2-based race car with a coupé body, heavily redesigned, featuring a slightly longer wheelbase and larger wheels and tyres. Built around a tubular space frame, the four-cylinder 1587cc boxer engine had four shaft-driven overhead camshafts and now produced 160 bhp. Weighing only 550kg, it had a top speed of about 225 km/h, which is still impressive today. Despite rule changes by the FIA, first time out the RS60 took everyone by surprise, blowing the competition into the weeds at Sebring with a Porsche one-two, totally obliterating the Ferraris that made up the rest of the points. The same car went on to win the Targa Florio again in 1960, with other RS60s also coming third and fifth between the inevitable Ferraris. (Some 36 years later, the winning car was flown by the Porsche factory

Right The Porsche 718 RS60 of Maurice Trintignant and Hans Herrmann, as it appeared at Le Mans before piston failure caused its retirement early in the race.

to Tasmania to compete in the Targa Tasmania 1996, driven by Jochen Mass, Le Mans winner for Porsche in 1989.)

The RS60s did not perform well at Le Mans, but were in points positions for most of the other races of the 1960 season. The German authorities helpfully decided to run their Grand Prix that year for Formula 2 cars rather than Formula 1, so the RS60s did particularly well there, with Graham Hill, Bonnier and the redoubtable Wolfgang ('Taffy') von Trips taking three of the top four places in what some argued was a rigged field (the other podium finisher was Jack Brabham's Cooper Climax). The following year's model, the RS61, did not impress though, and despite a healthy second and third in the Targa Florio was comprehensively beaten by the Ferraris throughout the season.

Another Spyder variant on the 718 was the WRS, constructed initially in 1961 as a four-cylinder model. A year later, fitted with a 2-litre flat-eight formation, it began to overtake the ailing RS61. While still outclassed by the Ferraris for the overall titles, it took important class victories not just in the great road races such as Le Mans and the Nürburgring, but also in hillclimbing, claiming the season's championship with Edgar Barth in 1963 and 1964 before it was retired to the Porsche Museum.

By the end of 1962 the sports car derivatives were no longer truly competitive for sports car racing. The last of the line – the 2-litre, eight-cylinder 718 GTR – recorded a final and historic Targa Florio win in 1963, but it was merely a blip: the 718's time in formula racing was up.

But there was always more to the adaptable little 718 than formula and sportscar racing. One of the 718 variations was the Bergspyder, a special version made to compete and win hillclimbs – hence the name – at which it proved phenomenally successful during the late 1950s to mid-1960s. Hillclimbing is a national institution in Germany, so Porsche's domination could possibly be expected, and during its most successful hillclimb period its successful drivers were almost exclusively Grand Prix men. In 1958 two such, Wolfgang von Trips and Jean Behra, fought an exhilarating battle for the IMSA hillclimb title, both in Porsche 718s. In 1960, 718s were placed first through fifth in the same championship; a stunning achievement for any manufacturer, let

Above *The 718 RSK of Jean Behra, who set up his own Behra Porsche racing team in 1959 after several successful seasons with the factory team.*

Below *Gerhardt Mitter, multiple IMSA champion for Porsche, takes another victory at a hillclimb in Freibourg in 1968 courtesy of the 718 Bergspyder.*

Right The No. 28 RS of Barth and Linge, shown mid-race at Le Mans in 1963, where it won its class and finished eighth overall.

alone one whose first model had appeared less than a decade before. They continued to achieve throughout the rest of the decade.

So it can be seen that 718s were raced by customers worldwide in a plethora of different championships. This helped both to enhance Porsche's reputation as an innovator and to make the race-watching and car-buying public aware of the Porsche name. From Le Mans to Sebring, the 718 in its various flavours dominated the racing world into the mid-1960s: a legendary car driven by now legendary heroes including Stirling Moss, Jean Behra, Jo Bonnier, Wolfgang von Trips and Dan Gurney, to name but a few. And these pretty little lightweight 718s were winning races whatever the opposition, even against the 3-litre Ferraris and Maseratis. With only 33 built, the 718s are today one of the rarest, most beautiful of the early Porsches, and are the spiritual predecessor of the present-day Type 986 (Boxster).

THE 904

The 904 was a landmark car for Porsche. It marked the end of the company's four-cylinder racing journey and, with its replacement by the 906 in 1966, the end of the road-racer genre at which Porsche had become so adept.

Like the 911, the 904 was designed by Butzi Porsche, Ferry's son. It did away with the 718's spaceframe chassis, reverting instead to a more old-fashioned ladder frame. However, Porsche had learned some useful tricks from British engineering stars like Cooper and Chapman, and the 904 had a sleek and swoopy glass-fibre body bonded straight on to the chassis. The result was not only light, it was extremely rigid. The original plan was for the 904 GTS to use a six-cylinder engine, but Porsche erred on the side of caution and used the Carrera four, which was known to be competitive and reliable. With all-round disc brakes, almost 200bhp and a 160mph potential, the 904 was a formidable car.

It took victory on its debut in the punishing Targa Florio in 1964 (a 904 also finished second), and won the 2-litre class at Le Mans the same year. In fact, all five 904s finished the

24-Hour race, placing seventh, eighth, tenth, eleventh and twelfth overall and further enhancing the Porsche reputation for reliability and pace. A class victory at La Sarthe followed in 1965, but the face of Porsche racing cars was about to change. Although the 904 was quick and specialized, it was still a racing road car, and these were still the days when people drove cars to an event, competed and drove back home. Once fitted with six- and eight-cylinder racing engines, the 904 ceased to be anything but a pure racer. With 220bhp and top speeds in excess of 170mph, it was no longer a car for the amateur. The limits of racing cars were stratospheric, and the sheer skill required to extract the maximum from them required a new breed of dedicated racing driver. The era of gentlemen racers and the direct development of road cars for racing purposes had come to an end.

Above *The privately-entered 904 GTS of Franc and Kerguen leads a Ferrari in the 1964 24 Heures du Mans. It took the 2-litre class win and finished eighth overall.*

Bottom left *Another 904 GTS from 1964, on show in Germany.*

This page *A 1969 example of the 917K in Gulf-Wyer racing colours, as used at Monza in 1971. The rear spoilers were originally added for CanAm racing, where cornering stability was all-important.*

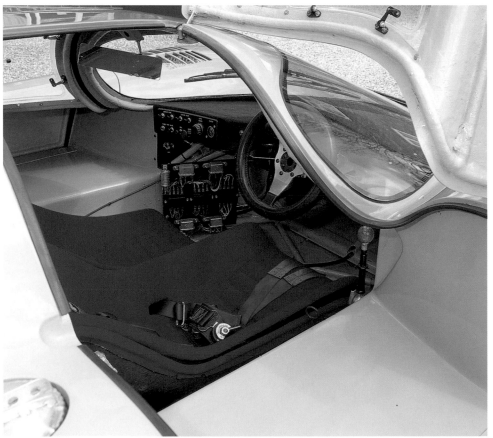

Porsche knew that to capitalize on its successes so far it needed to be competing and winning at the very highest levels. Class victories were no longer enough. This pursuit of outright victory accelerated the racing programme, and by 1966 the 904 was eclipsed. Within three years, Porsche would have its first legendary world beater: the 520bhp 917.

THE 917

Despite the success at class level, and the close second place in the 1968 race, Porsche had yet to claim an overall victory at La Sarthe after almost two decades of competing in the event. To rectify this situation, the company set out to construct a purpose-built racer to comply with upcoming regulations. The options were a 3-litre open-topped prototype or a 5-litre 'production' sports car. Porsche opted for the latter solution, and set about building 25 examples in order to homologate it. The result, designed by Ferdinand Piech, was the awesome 917, with a monstrous 4.5-litre flat-twelve engine that was over a metre long and produced 520bhp. It debuted at the Geneva Motor Show early in 1969 and left nobody in any doubt that Porsche were out to win Le Mans. Things didn't go to plan, though. The long-tailed bodywork intended for Le Mans wasn't ideal for the car's handling balance, and in the end both factory cars retired – though they were in the lead at the time – and the privately entered car crashed, killing its driver and team owner, John Woolfe.

In 1970 the 917K appeared, the 'K' standing for 'kurz', which referred to the shortened bodywork. With its upswept tail and modified front end supplying much-improved aerodynamic performance, the factory cars were unstoppable, coming first and second. The next year it was a similar story: the 917, now putting out more than 600bhp, romped to a Le Mans one-two for a second consecutive year, the winning car driven by Helmut Marko and Gijs van Lennep averaging a record-breaking 138mph. It is a testament to this great model that in this year, of 51 Le Mans entries 24 were Porsches, and a third of those 917s. Sales of Porsche's road cars received a hefty and welcome boost as a result of the car's track successes.

With the main objective accomplished, the 917s crossed the Atlantic to compete in the CanAm series. Here they lost their roofs, but gained twin turbochargers. They dominated the series in 1972, and again in 1973, by which time they were producing around 1100bhp and were capable of over 250mph.

Below The aerodynamic curves of the 1970 917 Spyder.

Bottom The Le Mans-winning 917K of Attwood and Herrmann, which headed a Porsche one-two-three in the famous event in 1970 and also took the lap record.

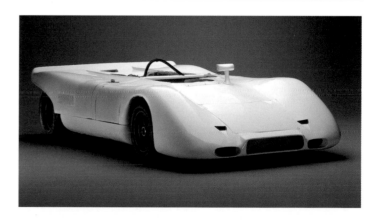

THE 935

In 1976, in an attempt to outlaw the 3-litre prototypes that had been dominating world sports car racing, the racing authorities introduced the World Championship of Makes. To comply with the regulations, cars were required only to retain the silhouette of the production model upon which they were based, as well as the engine block. Otherwise, they were a blank sheet of paper. The result from Porsche was the wild 935. In theory it was based upon the 2.1-litre Turbo Carrera from 1974, but by the time the boffins had finished it had a 590bhp 2.8-litre engine. Combined with the lurid aerodynamic addenda, the 935 was capable of topping 200mph.

Porsche took victory in that first Championship of Makes in a close-run duel with BMW, but by 1977 the 935s were packing twin-turbo power and an extra 40bhp, and they registered one-twos in every single round. But it wasn't until the following year, 1978, that the wildest 935 of all broke cover. Nicknamed 'Moby Dick' because of its whale-like bodywork extensions – the result of clever manipulation of the Group 5 regulations – it bore little resemblance to the 911. In fact, only the roof, roof pillars and door remained from the roadgoing car. With its engine capacity stretched to 3.2 litres and packing twin KKK turbochargers, Moby Dick boasted almost 850bhp at 8200rpm. The car was so light it required lead ballast, distributed carefully for optimum balance, to bring it up to the mandatory minimum weight limit.

Top Nicknamed 'Moby Dick' for its whale-like appearance, the 935/78 roared to success at Silverstone in 1978 but managed only eighth at Le Mans.

Above The only slightly less fanciful 1976 model of the 935.

Moby Dick handled superbly. At its Silverstone debut it won by seven laps, with an astonishing lap time close to that of contemporary Grand Prix cars. Victory at La Sarthe seemed assured, but a persistent misfire resulted in a lowly eighth spot. Fortunately, the 935 would have the success it deserved the following year, when a Kremer-entered 935 driven by Klaus Ludwig and Dale and Bill Whittington won the French classic, two other private 935s completing the top three.

THE 936

The open-cockpit 936 was designed specifically for Group 6 competition and proved hugely successful, netting three Le Mans wins including back-to-back victories in 1976 and 1977. Without the restriction of having to base the car on a roadgoing model, Porsche developed the chassis of the late-1960s 908, which had proved so successful in the Targa Florio long-distance races. It was powered by a 2142cc turbocharged version of the six-cylinder Boxer engine (based on that of the Turbo Carrera), tuned to give over 500bhp. Visually the car wasn't too far removed from the 917 CanAm racers of the early 1970s, though the huge air scoop above the driver's head rendered it easily distinguishable.

Porsche had entered two 936s in that 1976 Le Mans race, and though one retired, the winning car, driven by Gijs van Lennep and Jacky Ickx, triumphed by a massive eleven-lap margin. The 936 also took the World Sports car Championship that year, thanks to its winning

Left The Le Mans-winning Jules 936 of 1981, as driven by Ickx and Bell.

Below The Martini Porsche team of 1979, including Jacky Ickx, with the race-ready 935 and 936.

combination of massive performance and staggering reliability – only one retirement all season! By the time the 936s returned to La Sarthe in 1977 they had grown another turbocharger, but initially things didn't look good. Lead driver Ickx retired early, switching (as was the practice) to the other car which was running in a lowly fifteenth place. Ickx went on to drive like a man possessed, and by dawn the 936 was up to second. When the leading car dropped out, a famous victory seemed assured, but in the final hour disaster struck. Still, quick thinking by one of his co-drivers, Hurley Haywood, and good pit work allowed the car to rejoin the race and limp home to victory on just five cylinders.

The 1979 race saw all three 936s drop out, but Porsche's blushes were saved by the 935. In 1980, a 936 finished second, but better was to come the following year. Now with a 2.6-litre engine and piloted by two Le Mans legends, Derek Bell and Jacky Ickx, the 936 romped home to register Porsche's sixth triumph at the event.

Below The dial-laden cockpit of a racing 956.

Bottom One of the famous Skoal Bandit 956s of 1985, which took fourth at Le Mans under the control of David Hobbs, Jo Gartner and Guy Edwards.

THE 956

The 956, with its Formula One-derived 'ground effect' aerodynamics and famous Rothmans livery, is one of the most distinctive and successful Porsche racers of all time. Utilizing a monocoque chassis for the first time, Porsche built the 956 in compliance with the new Group C regulations. With around 630bhp from its mid-mounted 2.6-litre twin-turbo flat-six motor, the 956 could top 235mph on the Mulsanne and possessed fearsome cornering ability.

In 1982, with the indomitable Ickx and Bell once again sharing driving duties in the lead car, things were set fair, or perhaps that should be perfect, because the 956s obliterated the competition, taking first, second and third, Ickx recording a record-breaking sixth personal victory. The next year was even more incredible: the 956s filled the first eight places, Vern Schuppan, Hurley Haywood and Al Holbert at the wheel of the winning car. Even without a factory effort in 1984, the 956 remained

Left The innards of the 1985 model 956 uncovered.

unbeatable thanks to the efforts of Reinhold Joest's privateers. A certain Henri Pescarolo drove the winning car (alongside Klaus Ludwig), much to the delight of the French fans. Joest's success was repeated in 1985, despite the return of a works effort, and incredibly it was the same chassis (956/117) that took the chequered flag for the second successive time.

The 956's reign at the top of the Le Mans tree was broken in 1986, but only by the even more formidable 962. There was no denying the 956 had been a huge success. It had won Le Mans four times in a row and had totally dominated Group C and the World Endurance Championship. In 1984, 956s had won every single round. For many, the blue and white 956 will remain the definitive Porsche racing car.

THE 962

The 962 was not dissimilar, either visually or mechanically, to the 956. In fact, it first saw action in 1984 when the 956 was still very much in its heyday, dominating Le Mans and the World Endurance Championship. Instead of Europe, the 962 was designed for competition across the Atlantic. America was a crucial marketplace for Porsche, and the kudos to be gained from a successful motorsport campaign there could not be underestimated.

The US cars had different engine sizes, varying from 2.8 to 3.2 litres, but were restricted to only one turbocharger. They were, like the 956, exceptionally successful, winning 46 IMSA races between 1984 and 1987. The car's Le Mans glory was to come after the factory modified them for Group C compliance. With 3-litre engines, fully water-cooled and producing over 650bhp, the 962 could top 240mph, making it one of the fastest racing cars in history. Derek Bell, Hans Stuck and Al Holbert piloted a 962 to successive victories in both the Daytona and Le Mans 24-Hour races in 1986 and 1987. The 1987 win gave Porsche an incredible, and record-breaking, seven successive Le Mans victories.

Jaguar brought this astonishing run to a halt in 1988, but that was not the end of the 962 story. Somehow, six years later in 1994 two heavily modified Dauer 962s managed to

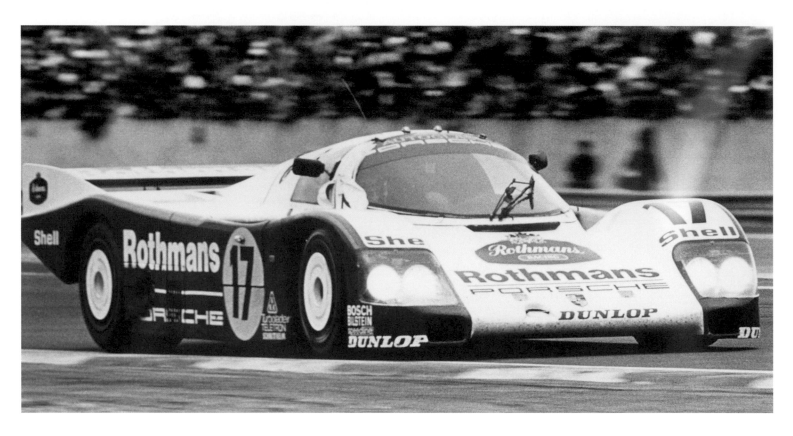

Above The No. 17 Rothmans Porsche 962C of Hans-Joachim Stuck, Derek Bell and Al Holbert retook the Le Mans crown in 1987.

manipulate regulations to gain access to the grand touring (GT) class. The 962 not only won its class but also took first and third places overall, notching up Porsche's thirteenth win in the process. Quite a swansong.

THE GT1 AND TWR SPYDER

The GT1 might well be the most expensive, radical and breathtaking road car in the company's history, but it only ever saw public roads in order to homologate the wild GT-class contender for Le Mans. Under the complicated rules of the Sarthe circuit at the time, an entrant could build and enter almost anything for the great race, so long as it was approved for the street by one of the sport's governing bodies.

Although carrying the 911 moniker, and resembling the 911 in overall shape, what Singer's team created was unique. While the front, from the cowl forward, consisted of the 933 model 911's inner sheet metal structure, from there on back it was a pure competition vehicle, using technology quite similar to that of the 956/963. Even its water-cooled Boxer six-cylinder engine had its origins in that car's powerplant.

Still, some at Porsche were worried that the 911 GT1 was too untried to win at Le Mans on its first time out, and they began looking for alternatives. Enter the Walkinshaw Spyder, or TWRS. This former group-C prototype, built first as a Jaguar by Walkinshaw in 1991 and later turned into a Mazda, of all things, was sold to the Zuffenhausen concern after Porsche's 1994 Le Mans victory. They cut off its roof, made a few other adjustments to meet the new World Sports Car prototype regulations, and installed a Porsche 956/962 water-cooled and turbo-charged flat-six, with the intent of going back to Le Mans. However, regulations changes again foiled the team, and eventually the Spyders were leased to Reinhold Joest to run at Le Mans as a back-up for the 911 GT1 effort in 1996.

Although Porsche made much of the fact the the GT1 had won the GT1 class, and the 911s the GT2 class, the real glory, and outright victory, went to the little Spyder, the two factory GT1s

being forced to settle for second and third overall. The GT1 returned to action later that year in the BPR Global Endurance GT challenge, winning three events of that series' final year (It was replaced in 1997 by the FIA GT championship).

This led to a series of customer 911 GT1 replicas being produced, offering 600bhp and vying for the title of fastest road car ever made – although with a price tag of almost £500,000 they were available to a select few and unlikely to be spotted in the local car park. Meanwhile the factory entered the updated 911 GT1 'Evo' at Le Mans and in the FIA GT championship. Mercedes

thrashed them in the FIA title but the factory GT1s were looking good at Le Mans until mechanical failure ended their run in the final laps – ironically leaving the way open for the privately entered Joest Porsche TWR Spyder, driven by Michele Alboreto, Stefan Johansson and Tom Kristensen, to again take over for the win.

But Porsche was not to be denied in its fiftieth anniversary year, and the GT1s got their own back in 1998. Totally revised, the 1998 chassis was pure carbon fibre and the aerodynamics were almost unrecognizable. They were still outclassed in the FIA GT championship, but stormed Le Mans with Allan McNish, Stéphane Ortelli and Laurent Aiello at the controls to claim a last-gasp one-two overall. It was a fitting birthday present for Professor Porsche.

The GT1s were then retired, with the TWR Spyder, to the famous Porsche museum, from which they would occasionally emerge to compete in classic meetings. At least that was the plan, but in fact the 911 GT1s weren't finished yet. Porsche sold one of the Evos to the American-based concern Champion Racing, who drove it successfully to win the 1998 United

Top *German brewer Warsteiner have long been sponsors of Porsche racing, including the GT1 teams of 1996 who were just pipped to the post at Le Mans by the TWR Spyder of Joest Racing.*

Bottom *The Kremer Porsche K8 of 1995 as driven by Laessig, Konrad and Herrmann at Le Mans. They retired after 16 hours but team-mates Stuck, Bouchut and Boutsen finished sixth overall.*

Below A typical example of the 3.8-litre 993-generation 911 'Cup' cars used in Carrera Cup and Porsche Supercup racing.

Bottom A Porsche 911 Carrera competing in the Monte Carlo rally of 1979.

States Road Racing Championship series GT title, plus the GT division at the 'Petit Le Mans' event in the new American Le Mans Series. And in 2001 the GT1 was invited by the US governing body to return to active competition in the American Road Racing Championship, as well as the classic and historic meetings for which it is more than qualified.

THE 911

In an age of ultra-high-technology four-wheel-drive rally specials, it's easy to forget that Porsche has a proud and successful rallying heritage, with no fewer than four outright victories in the Monte Carlo rally as well as two wins with the 959 in the gruelling Paris–Dakar rally-raid.

Before Audi came along and changed rallying for ever with the Quattro four-wheel-drive system, traction was the name of the game in traditionally snowy, icy events like the 'Monte', and the 911 held a trump card. With its engine slung way back over the rear wheels, resulting in a tail-heavy weight distribution, the Porsche had more mass over its driven rear wheels and so dug into the snow and ice much better than front-engined rivals. That mass at the rear also gave the 911 the ability to change direction with startling agility, swinging from corner to corner using the pendulous tail as an ally rather than the enemy it could sometimes prove to be when it came to traditional road use. The 911 was also extremely tough, and on events that lasted far longer and covered many more miles than modern rallies, this told. Porsche also had the advantage of a fantastic driver, and future World Rally champion, Bjørn Waldegaard. It was Waldegaard who took the 911 to victory in the wintery Monte Carlo and Swedish rallies in both 1969 and 1970.

THE 959

With a reputation already acquired at Le Mans for dominating the world's toughest motor races, what better way to back this up than by tackling the Paris–Dakar rally-raid? Covering up to 9000 miles in just 22 days across the most demanding of terrains, the Paris–Dakar made La Sarthe look like a picnic.

The 959 rally project grew out of the existing 911 SC RS programme and 1982's new Group B regulations. Three heavily revised 911s fitted with an early version of the 959's four-wheel-drive transmission and run by the Prodrive team entered the 1984 Paris–Dakar and recorded a surprise win with Dominique Lemoyne and René Metge at the helm.

Surely the far more advanced 959 that was to follow would be all-conquering? That was certainly the plan. The 959 was intended to be an off-road equivalent of the unstoppable 962 Le Mans racer. It had a twin-turbo flat-six engine with the potential to produce up to 600bhp. It also featured a ground-breaking six-speed gearbox and electronically controlled four-wheel-drive system. The 959 was arguably the most advanced rally car of its time. Buoyed by that 1984 success, a trio of 959s entered the 1985 event, but the factory hadn't finished the twin-turbo engines in time and the cars were hamstrung by having to use less powerful 911 engines. All three retired. It wasn't until later in 1985, in the Egyptian 'Pharaoh's Rally', that the 959 recorded its first rallying success.

By the time the Rothmans-liveried machines returned to the desert in 1986, the programme was in trouble. Dave Richards and his Prodrive team had grown tired of constant factory delays holding up the car's development and the lack of results the project had yielded. Stir in a worldwide economic slowdown and the fact that each of the 200 road cars Porsche had to build for homologation purposes was rumoured to be costing the company twice its £150,000-plus list price, and the 959 seemed doomed. Victories in the 1986 event and the 1000 Pistes rally later in the same year were just too little too late. Porsche's plans for domination of the world of rallying finally died when Henri Toivinan's fatal crash at Corsica caused the FIA to pull the plug on the Group B class.

Top The 959 in familiar Rothmans/Shell livery. The model had mixed success but eventually took a one-two at the Paris–Dakar in 1986.

Bottom The engine of the rallying 959.

END OF THE ROAD?

The 959s and GT1s can be considered the last of the 'true great' Porsches to be manufactured entirely by the German concern for race use against other marques. Later models such as the GT2 were influential of course, as were the various 911 derivatives developed for the Porsche-only Supercup and Carrera Cup series, and the 944 Turbo and Boxster which were, of course, extensively raced by privateers – but these were not run for big-budget factory-sponsored teams with the intention of taking on the manufacturing competition and thoroughly thrashing them. The factory took part in collaborations with other designers, engineers and manufacturers in, for example, the creation of the triple-winning McLaren Formula 1 cars of the mid-1980s, but in these they were generally not creating an entire package of chassis-plus-engine to race spec and entering their own exclusive teams. The high ongoing costs of both developing race-tuned motors and running efficient, adaptable race teams – and the small returns other than in publicity value – were just not cost-efficient enough for Zuffenhausen. It didn't stop the enthusiasts, but the glory days of the cash-rich factory teams were no more.

chapter
ten

The Sporting Heritage

A few statistics may help the uninitiated to understand the massive impact Porsche has had on the world racing scene at the highest level. Le Mans 24-Hour – sixteen outright victories; Daytona 24-Hour – eighteen outright victories; Sebring 12-Hour – seventeen outright victories; Targa Florio – eleven outright victories; Formula 1 (with McLaren) – three world championships. And that's before mention is made of the four Monte Carlo rally wins, two more in the Paris–Dakar race and no fewer than fourteen makes and team championship titles. Then there's a further twenty IMSA (European Hillclimb Championship) titles, and numerous other victories in national and class racing. In fact, this relatively small marque has recorded well over 23,000 victories in all competitions, making it by far the most successful car manufacturer in international racing. And that number is growing by the year. There are events that Porsche has dominated almost to the exclusion of all others; and here we look at them, and at some of the drivers that have succeeded for Porsche throughout the years.

THE EVENTS PORSCHE MADE ITS OWN

As we have seen above there are some events at which Porsche have particularly excelled: the long-distance Italian road races; the strength-sapping team endurance races; the hillclimbs at which the Germans are the renowned experts; rallying in all kinds of conditions. Let us not underestimate the effect of this racing pedigree of Porsche's on the reputation and sales of its road cars. The old adage 'win on Sunday, sell on Monday' couldn't be truer than with Porsche. Even today, with the 911 GT2 road car, race-driven technology such as the ceramic brake disc is being used to give the buyer unrivalled performance on the road. There may not have been the high-profile factory-backed assaults on Le Mans or Formula 1 recently, but 2001 saw Porsche build a record number of 911 racing cars for use in the American Le Mans Series and Porsche Supercup, which suggests the company's racing heritage remains in good hands.

Previous page Early days: one of the first 356 Carreras takes a break during the Rallye des Alpes.

Below The 356B 2000GS of Gerhardt Koch and Carel de Beaufort rounds a turn at Le Mans in 1963, hotly pursued by team-mates Heinz Schiller and Ben Pon.

Le Mans, along with the Monaco Grand Prix and the Indianapolis 500, is still one of the world's most famous motor races. First run on the local roads of the town in 1923, which were later incorporated into the now-infamous Sarthe circuit, the 24 Heures du Mans is credited by many as having a huge influence on the development of the sports car, together with its then Italian counterpart, the Mille Miglia. The two races, both designed to test to the limit the endurance of both car and drivers (three per team) over 24 hours, played a large part in the formation of the World Sports Car Championship in 1953, and were together considered by many the main events of the championship season until the latter was discontinued in 1957, partly for safety reasons. The authorities at Le Mans eventually pulled out of the championship in 1976 following a spat with the FIA over various changes to the regulations which meant that only true in-production cars were allowed to compete, not the 'sporting prototypes' that the French had allowed since the end of World War II. The admission of such prototypes (which had to achieve homologation as potential road models by at least one appropriate authority to be allowed to compete) had allowed both Porsche and Ferrari to win using models that would otherwise have been disallowed, and had given all manufacturers the chance to test such types in a class of their own. To this day, the race still attracts crowds of up to 250,000 in this age where most motorsport events are overshadowed by the hype of Formula 1.

The Porsche love affair with this French endurance classic dates back over half a century to 1951, when a Porsche 356 claimed victory in the 1100cc class. It took another 19 years for them to achieve the overall title, but in the following decades Porsche went on to become the event's most successful entrants with an unmatched number of outright victories, which included a run of seven successive wins between 1981 and 1987 (see below). The same could have been true of the late 1960s and early 1970s, had they not been battling with the mighty Ferraris, with whom they often shared the top three places. Throughout its time at Le Mans Porsche has also notched up dozens of class wins and the ubiquitous 911 still dominates the production-orientated class each year.

Porsches similarly dominate the American endurance classics: Daytona and Sebring have each had more than their share of Porsches in the top three, and from their earliest days of racing the 356s were winning classes there. As part of the World Sports Car Championship these successes have helped build towards Porsche's many titles in this field of racing. With

Above *The Martini-sponsored 917 of Helmut Marko and Gijs van Lennep leads – and later wins – at Le Mans in 1971.*

Top *A Porsche 550 Spyder competes in a round of the IMSA European hillclimb championship in 1962.*

Bottom *The 908/30 of Leo Kinnunen and Pedro Rodriguez finishes second in the Targa Florio of 1970. The race was won by team-mates Jo Siffert and Brian Redman in an identical car.*

the new American Le Mans series just getting into its stride, there can be no doubt that Porsches will continue to honour their endurance heritage with many more podium finishes.

Success has also come in events that blur the boundaries between road and racetrack, with cars that are as much road machine as race specialist. The Targa Florio, one of the most sought-after title claims on any racedriver's or manufacturer's list, ran from 1906 to 1973 on various road-based and banked tracks in Sicily. Still considered a classic and defining event, it attracted teams from across the world and was rivalled only by its mainland counterpart and Le Mans in status. Starting in 1951, Porsche won it more times than any other manufacturer or team: eleven in total, plus eight second places and ten third. In 1959, 1967 and 1969 they took all three podium places. Since 1973 the race has continued to be run, but for safety reasons at a more sedate pace, and is altogether a tamer event. It was dropped from the World Sports Car Championship for this reason, but Porsches still compete, although no longer as a factory-sponsored team.

Hillclimbing is a little-publicized sport outside mainland Europe, but it has a devout following and is particularly popular in Germany, Porsche's home of course. Maybe it is for this reason that the Porsche teams scored so well at these events: some 20 European hillclimb championship titles, plus numerous second and third places and individual event wins. Until 1962 the cars used were inevitably unmodified 550 Spyders, but after a crushing defeat by Ferrari that year Porsche began to develop cars specifically for this type of event, first putting its 771 flat-eight engine into a UK-built Elva, and then adapting the 904 coupés and WRSs to suit the job in hand. They didn't quite measure up to the awesome Ferraris though, so Piech then designed an all-new, tube-framed topless model, the Ollon-Villars Spyder, now considered the godfather of all racing Porsches. It weighed in at only 500kg and allowed Porsche to totally dominate the sport throughout 1968, despite handling problems. By the end of the year Porsche had redeveloped the car into the 909, then further refinements brought the unbeatable 910. Successes were still pouring in, but at the end of the 1969 season Porsche ended the factory association with hillclimbing to concentrate solely on sports car racing. Privateers continue to race a wide range of Porsche models, but the factory team has never returned to this venerable sport, which deserves more attention than it gets from the sports media.

Rallying is another of Porsche's fortes; not only the familiar mudbath version we witness each year in the UK as part of today's RAC rally but snow rallying in Scandinavia; long-distance

Left *A Dutch competitor in the Monte Carlo rally of 1959 shows off his Porsche 356B.*

Bottom *Alain Prost at Monaco on the way to his eighteenth Grand Prix win and the 1986 Formula 1 title, in the McLaren-TAG MP4/2B with Porsche-designed engine*

desert treks such as the famous Paris–Dakar and Safari events; and the more 'road-based' invitation races such as the Monte Carlo dash. Porsches have won them all, repeatedly, and continue to do so, both as factory-sponsored teams and the cars of choice for many a privateer.

The Monte Carlo rally, held annually since the 1920s and sporadically for a decade before, is a unique event whereby cars start from several different points across Europe and race to the principality of Monaco against each other and the clock. Originally a test that included a focus on reliability and driver comfort as well as speed, these days it incorporates various special stages of pure flat-out racing as well as the highway-based sections. Porsche's history here started early, and they have continued to score repeatedly, with the 1978 victory in particular demonstrating their abilities. In an especially snow-bound event, which caused havoc among many of the more powerful of the field and left most teams struggling for grip,

the privately-entered Carrera of Jean-Pierre Nicholas and Vincent Laverne stormed through to take victory, leaving the Ferrari-inspired Lancias bereft. Some ten years earlier, the factory team of Vic Elford and David Stone had clinched Porsche's first title there in a Porsche 911T in similar circumstances.

So why does Porsche not feature in the international carnival that is Formula 1 in the 21st century? After all, Porsche has had some exciting F1 history: from the early 1960s it competed in many events using an eight-cylinder air-cooled engine in a revised 804 model. But they took only one win, with Dan Gurney at the French Grand Prix of 1962, and the car was never as technically advanced as its competitors, having, for example, traditional carburettors and steel-rimmed wheels rather than the fuel-injection and lightweight alloys favoured by the Lotus team and others. It has been suggested that this was the result of restrictions on the team's budget by Ferry Porsche, who was highly sceptical of the whole F1 'experiment'. More experience and commitment would have done wonders for the programme, but sports car racing was always more Ferry's style in those days, and they soon decided to concentrate their track efforts solely on that and quit Formula 1.

Porsche engines made a return to F1 in the 1980s of course, underpinning McLaren's mind-blowing carbon fibre Barnard-designed MP4/2 with a brand-new Metzger-designed, water-cooled 1.5-litre V6 turbo, paid for by the TAG organization. It won the British team and their German engine-makers three world championships. In 1984 the McLarens were virtually unbeatable, taking twelve out of the fifteen wins available with Lauda and Prost, and the latter secured the title for himself in 1985 and again in 86. Porsche further tweaked the engine the following year, but McLaren's car proved less reliable and a further win escaped them. In 1988 the British team switched to an engine deal with Honda, and Porsche was out of Formula 1 for the second time. Later collaboration with the Arrows/Footwork team in 1991 yielded little and cost much, and the engines were dropped by the struggling team mid-season. These days Porsche seems content to leave this most celebrated of series to the likes of Ferrari and its fellow countrymen BMW and Mercedes.

Similarly, Indianapolis and its accompanying CART championship have never been happy hunting grounds for Porsche. It did supply cars and engines on several occasions, with a view to competing – first, in 1979, in partnership with Ted Fields' Interscope team. Porsche announced it would supply for the following season a modified version of its traditional, water-cooled, flat-six-cylinder turbo to be used in an Interscope chassis and driven by Danny 'On the gas' Ongais. But it came to nothing: the project was cancelled the following spring when the US Auto Club suddenly changed the rules and made the turbo invalid. Porsche withdrew, but returned some eight years later offering a Metzger V8 that used much of the technology of the TAG-sponsored Formula 1 engines. However, the Porsche chassis that accompanied it was uncompetitive and by the start of the following season the team was forced to switch to a March-built open-wheeler, retaining the same engine. They struggled on until the end of the 1990 season but won only once, despite having the best driver, Teo Fabi, and one of the most reliable and powerful engines on the grid. It just wasn't to be.

RACING HEROES – THE MEN AND THEIR VICTORIES

Race-bred Porsches have been driven in a variety of motorsport series by a huge number of drivers – some of them major stars – both independent and factory-contracted. Indeed, to have the latest sports Porsche waiting for you on the grid, in the pits, behind the start-line rope or at the bottom of a challenging hill appears to have always been an attractive proposition for any aspiring champion. Here we present some of those, both the famous and the near-forgotten, whose names should feature most prominently on Porsche's roll of sporting honour. The machines they drove were certainly legends. But so should their drivers be considered, for their courage, enthusiasm and all-round skill and dedication.

Opposite page

Top *The 1962 French Grand Prix, which Dan Gurney won in the No. 30 Porsche 804 – the first Porsche Grand Prix success.*

Bottom *Huschke von Hanstein (standing) takes notes from Jo Bonnier at the German Grand Prix of 1962. Bonnier is driving the 804 F8.*

Below *Auguste Veuillet and Edmon Mouche take Porsche's first class victory at Le Mans in the 356/4. They finished twentieth overall.*

__Right__ The RSK owned by Jean Behra and raced by the drivers of his own Behra Racing team – while he was driving the same races for the Ferrari team!

__Below__ Porsche 550 RS Spyder of Richard von Frankenburg and Helmut Polensky takes a class win at Le Mans in 1955, and finishes fourth overall.

Early days: 1950–60

It all started in the 1950s, shortly after production of the 356 had begun in earnest (see chapter 4). Their first entrants were often independent wealthy enthusiasts, often introduced by the larger-than-life Racing Director and Press Officer Huschke von Hanstein, a former professional racing and test driver who in the early days added himself to the teamsheet whenever he felt like it. He had a lot of well-connected racing friends to whom he recommended, and sold, the latest racing Porsche models, which then appeared in a variety of series. He was also responsible for building many of the successful factory teams – and for publicizing them, of course.

The first recorded victory was a class win at Le Mans by Auguste Veuillet (Porsche's French importer) and Edmon Mouche in 1951. The Gmünd 356 coupé was the only Porsche entered, as the second car was damaged in practice. The standard 1086cc, 40bhp engine and bodywork allowed the car to reach a top speed of 88mph. By giving each wheel covers to reduce airflow disturbance and boosting the engine to 46bhp the race version was capable of 100mph. Records show the little Porsche bested the track for a lap average of 87.3mph and they finished 20th overall.

This was followed a few months later by an even more impressive achievement. The long-distance, 91-hour Liège–Rome–Liège rally was an incredible test of endurance for both man and machine. Crisscrossing Europe non-stop, including the hairy mountain passes of the Alps, it took guts and determination. Porsche had supported this event from the beginning with factory cars, and it paid off in 1952 when Helmut Polensky and his partner Walter Schluter won the event outright, also in a Gmünd coupé. This was stunning: competing against English and Italian sports cars with more than twice the cubic capacity, it proved beyond doubt the Porsche's durability, manoeuvrability, and adaptability to mountain runs. The same year the team won the equally demanding Alpine and Sestrière rallies, and a year later Polensky and Schluter took the European rally title for Porsche.

Also in 1953, José Herrarte won a class victory (up to 1550cc) at the fearsome Carrera Panamericana. A year later in 1954, the final year of this great race, Hans Herrmann took the class win in a 550 Spyder and also achieved an incredible third place overall – only the massive power of the two 5-litre Ferraris could beat him. Another class win was forthcoming at Le Mans, soon to be Porsche's favoured event, with factory drivers Richard von Frankenburg and Paul Frere in a 550 coupé. Meanwhile the 356s continued to take class wins by the handful, from Monza and Belgrade to the ice-race at Zell-am-See, Austria.

By now, Herrmann, Polensky, Edgar Barth, Helmut Glockner and Umberto Maglioli were Porsche's main drivers, with a number of others running in lower-profile rallies and endurance trials. Herrmann and Polensky teamed up at Le Mans but retired from engine failure, as did the other factory entry of von Frankenburg/Glockner. It wasn't a particularly productive year, although the team won various class titles in rally events, but in 1955 von Frankenburg won the German Sports Car Championship for the Stuttgart-based team, and took another class victory at Le Mans with Polensky.

By 1956 Porsche were in contention at the very top, winning the Targa Florio in style, with Maglioli and von Hanstein taking the honours. It is rumoured that Maglioli was given the drive – in a 550A, a car of only 130bhp but which weighed in at a slender 515kg – merely days before the start by Ferry Porsche himself. Maglioli and Barth competed in that year's German Grand Prix alongside the Porsche of private entrant Carel de Beaufort, with Barth winning the F2 class. He remained with the team for the following year, joined by Jean Behra. Now driving the RSK, Behra won at Reims and Avus in 1958 before leaving the factory team to develop his own version of the RSK, although sadly the following year he was fatally injured at the same circuit while driving in a preview race for the German Grand Prix.

Behra was replaced at Porsche by Wolfgang von Trips, with Jo Bonnier and Graham Hill among those completing the team in 1959, but they had little major success other than the one big one – Porsche's sensational top-four factory team victory at the Targa Florio, then a World Championship event. Meanwhile, Barth (who'd partnered Wolfgang Siedel to the Targa win) was dominating the European Mountain championship and won it that year for Porsche: a feat he was to repeat twice more, in 1963 and 1964.

Moving on up: the 1960s

With the new decade came another new face: with von Trips being snatched by Ferrari the Formula 1 team place went to Herrmann, who drove a number of 718 versions including the RS60, with which he took the Targa Florio crown, partnered by Bonnier and with Gendebien coming in third. Oddly this year it was generally the non-works Porsches that fared better: by this time the 718 chassis was being supplied to many private Formula 2 entrants including Rob Walker, whose driver was Stirling Moss, and the Equipe Nationale Belge team, which ran Olivier Gendebien when he wasn't working for the factory team. The most convincing victory

Left Dan Gurney competes in the British Grand Prix at Aintree in 1962, driving a Porsche 804. He finished ninth.

Above *The Porsche 904 of Antonio Pucci and Colin Davis rounds a Sicilian corner in 1964 on its way to another Targa Florio win.*

was a one-two-three in the BARC 200 at Aintree that year, with Moss first for Walker and Bonnier and Hill second and third in factory cars. Further Formula 2 success followed at the German GP (that year run exclusively for F2 cars), when the factory team scored first and fourth with Bonnier and Hill, and von Trips came second in a private Porsche -- all three were 718 derivatives. Hill scored two further sports car class wins for Porsche that year – with Barth in the Targa Florio and alone at Goodwood (in a 356 Carrera) – but overall victories were lacking.

Now eligible for F1, the 718-based RS61s looked a cert for the 1961 season, and Porsche kept Bonnier and Herrmann and, with the departure of Hill, added American Dan Gurney as third factory driver (who met his future wife, Evi, working for the formidable Baron von Hanstein in the Porsche Press department). But the team and its cars did not live up to expectations, although Gurney scored three second places during the season that placed him joint third in the championship with Moss. They were even pipped to the post in the Targa Florio by Ferrari, although Porsches finished second (Gurney/Bonnier) and third (Barth/Herrmann). In 1962 the RS61s were passed on to willing privateers, with the Porsche AG factory team driving the all-new 804. Gurney won his, and Porsche's, first F1 race – the French Grand Prix – at Rouen and one week later Gurney and Bonnier pulled a one-two out of the bag at Stuttgart, but there was little else for the team to celebrate that year. Then new regulations were introduced and Porsche withdrew from Formula racing to concentrate on sports car racing instead.

Bonnier again won the Targa Florio for them in 1963, with Carlo Abarte, and they also took third (Barth/Herbert Linge). In 1964 it was a Porsche 904 that took the chequered flag, this time under the expert hands of Antonio Pucci and Colin Davis; in 1965 Porsche missed out to Ferrari but finished third in a 904 driven by Linge and Maglioli and were back the following year with a race-winning 906 Carrera 6, driven by Herbert Müller and Willy Mairesse.

It all seemed to come together with the 907 in 1968: Porsches won at Daytona (Vic Elford/Jochen Neerpasch/Jo Siffert/Rolf Stommelen); Sebring 12-hr (Herrmann/Siffert); the Nürburgring 1000 (Elford/Siffert); and the Targa Florio (Maglioli again, in his final race, with Elford). The latter was becoming almost predictable – indeed would have been had it not been for the Ferraris. It was a trend that would continue until the early 1970s, with Porsche and Ferrari

battling it out for the top spot each year until the nifty Alfa Romeos roared away with it in 1971.

In 1969, sports cars ruled, and particularly Porsches. The 908 of Siffert and Redman won five rounds of the WSC Championship, ably supported by Elford and Kurt Ahmens. Meanwhile, the little 718 Bergspyders continued to storm the hillclimb charts with a variety of drivers. One of the sport's most tragic days occurred at Rossfeld in 1968, when Ludovico Scarfiotti – a seasoned campaigner of both hillclimb and Formula 1, who had in 1962 snatched the IMSA title for Ferrari from under Porsche's nose – lost control of his Bergspyder and slammed off the road into a clump of trees, dying instantly. Throttle problems were blamed for the accident, but stories abound that Scarfiotti, suffering badly after the recent death of friend and former team-mate Lorenzo

Bandini, had deliberately driven off the road to his death to avoid further injuring another competitor, who had crashed moments before and was lying in the road unable to move.

In rallying Porsche also enjoyed success in the 1960s, first with the Carrera driven by Hans-Joachim Walter and later with the 911, with Vic Elford winning the Tour de Corse in 1967 and the GT class at the Monte Carlo rally with David Stone. A year later the two men won the Monte Carlo event outright, followed home by another Porsche driver, Pauli Toivonen, who went on to become the European Champion. New signing Bjørn Waldegaard retained the trophy for Porsche in 1969, also winning the Swedish rally, another ice-and-snow extravaganza, the same year.

Top Bjorn Waaldegard on his way to Monte Carlo to claim another rally title in 1969.

Bottom The No. 23 Porsche 917 of Schutz and Mitter makes an appearance at Le Mans in 1969. Team mate Vic Elford, in No. 12, scored the fastest lap of the competition, but neither car finished the race.

Top The Martini-sponsored 917L of Gerard Larrousse and Vic Elford is pursued by an identical model in Gulf Wyer colours at Le Mans in 1971. The race was won by the other Martini Porsche of Helmut Marko and Gijs van Lennep.

Bottom The 917/10 was developed for CanAm racing (note the open cockpit) but proved equally useful in the Interserie. This is the 1973 model used by Leo Kinnunen.

The Seventies

It was the start of a roll for Porsche: the stupendous 917 added further titles in 1970 with an outright Le Mans victory for Herrmann and Attwood in the Porsche Salzburg team (owned by Louise Piech) and the World Endurance Championship – the first of many. It is a testament to this great model that in this year, of 51 entries to Le Mans, 24 were Porsches and a third of those 917s. In this celebrated year Porsche also won its first World Championship for Makes (manufacturers/constructors); the Targa Florio went to Siffert and Redman in the 908; and the team also had many successes in CanAm, TransAm and IMSA, with some of the best media exposure going to Steve McQueen's second place at Sebring (with Peter Revson) in a Porsche 908. For the third time in a row the Monte Carlo rally was won by Waldegaard in a 911S. It was all getting almost predictable.

1971 saw Porsche repeat its Le Mans victory, with Helmut Marko and Gijs van Lennep taking the top spot in the new Martini Porsche, averaging a record-breaking 138mph. Ahrens and Elford took the Nürburgring 1000 for the third time in a row, and the latter paired up with Larrouse to take Sebring in a 917K. The trophy cabinet in Zuffenhausen must have been the envy of many a manufacturer by this time. Not content to restrict themselves to the mostly European-based sports car series, the factory entered 917/10s for the CanAm series under the L&M racing banner – and came first and third.

The Zuffenhausen team had been sending cars to the series since 1969 at the urging of its North American racing boss, Josef Hoppen. Using a topless version of the Le Mans car, Jo Siffert drove it to fourth place in final point standings two years running and their interest was piqued. Unfortunately, the Swiss driver was killed in 1971 in a Formula 1 accident so didn't get to witness the 1972 win – the first of several years at which his team would dominate this event. Neither did the expected driver Mark Donohue, who was injured in testing and had to watch substitute George Follmer take the honours instead, alongside numerous privateers racing non-turbo 917s. These included Peter Gregg, racing for the rival Brumos Porsche team that he owned, who was placed third in the first of many McLaren/Porsche sandwiches. A prolific winner – over 41 races in the United States GTU and GTO series alone – Porsche fans were to see a lot more of him in the years to come, including four IMSA GT championship titles.

Donohue returned in 1973 with a revised model, the 917/30, fighting it out with the 917 privateers in the early rounds before steaming ahead mid-season. Sadly, at the end of 1973 Porsche were forced to withdraw from the series following new regulations on fuel supply, which it seemed would force the 917 to race at noncompetitive boost pressures. It returned only briefly, at the Mid-Ohio event in 1974 under the experienced hands of Redman, where it finished a surprising second. Meanwhile Porsche returned its 917s to Europe and the Interserie, winning the 1974 and 1975 championships. Not to be outdone, the 911 RSR won Daytona and many of the other IMSA events in the now famous Brumos colours, while Peter Gregg beat team-mate Al Holbert, both in Carrera RSRs, to the line to take the Trans-Am championship. To seal their place in history, van Lennep and Müller romped home in the last 'official' Targa Florio in a Carrera RSR, to retain Porsche's favourite title for eternity.

Also in this great year, Porsche completed a convincing coup: taking the top three places at Silverstone in the Interserie championship with 917/10 Turbos in the hands of the great Leo Kinnunen, Willy Kauhsen and Georg Loos, with Ernst Kraus and Gunter Stekkonig not far behind in the un-turboed version for fourth and sixth. The drivers represented a total of four teams, with two cars – Kauhsen's and Stekkonig's – being part of Kauhsen's own team in its first season. It followed a year in which Kinnunen and Kauhsen, each driving for a different Porsche team, were constantly battling for supremacy in an often-thrilling series. The result itself was somewhat reminiscent of the Nürburgring 1000 of 1971, when Porsches were so dominant that only four other cars featured in the top twenty finishers.

Throughout the mid-1970s Porsches continued to dominate both sports car and rally events and championships, with wins and drivers too many to list comprehensively. The double World Championship in a 935 and a 936 (group 5 and 6) must rank as a high achievement, as did the 1977 Le Mans win, which boasted a family connection: Jurgen Barth, son of early Porsche driver Edgar, who had become a Porsche factory sports car driver a few years before but celebrated his first major victory as part of the Sarthe-winning team of Jacky Ickx and Hurley Haywood. There's a story behind that win: early problems in Ickx's 936 (shared with Henri Pescarolo) had ended his race, so he offered to help out by sharing the team's second car of Haywood and Barth, then lying fifteenth. Ickx drove like never before and the entire team outdid themselves to take the lead close to the end. Ickx then suggested that Jurgen take the last lap – driving by now on five cylinders – to experience the win to its fullest. No wonder they made him an honorary citizen of Le Mans.

Meanwhile, prolific rally winner Jean-Pierre Nicholas added a fourth 911 win on the Monte Carlo in 1978 in the 936/78 Turbo in Martini racing colours, while in the US Redman, Garretson

Top *The turbo-powered Carrera RSR of Herbert Müller and Gijs van Lennep races to second place at Le Mans in 1974.*

Bottom *Five years on, another 911 Carrera powers its way to Monte Carlo in the wintry conditions of 1979.*

and Charles Mendez shot to victory in Sebring in the Porsche 935. The arrival of Klaus Ludwig towards the end of the decade led to two German Racing Championship titles, several endurance wins and another Le Mans win in the 925 in 1979 during particularly wet weather. A few years later he returned after a spell with Ford to win the Sarthe event hands-down in 1984 and 85 for the Joest–Porsche team.

1980s: F1 success at last

1981 saw Porsche finally getting its feet under the table of the Formula 1 World Championship, when McLaren supremo Ron Dennis asked the Stuttgart-based manufacturer to build a turbo-charged Formula 1 engine. Porsche told him to come back when he'd found the money to develop it. Luckily for them, Dennis managed to convince TAG to invest some £3m in the development of a 1.5-litre V6 Turbo, and so the Porsche-TAG engine was born. It was launched into the series at the Dutch Grand Prix in 1983 and the following year the excellent driver team of Nikki Lauda and Alain Prost totally dominated the World Championship, scoring twelve wins in sixteen races, with Lauda World Drivers' Champion and McLaren walking away with the Constructors' title. In 1985 they won six times and took both titles again, but by 1986 the Williams-Honda engines were becoming increasingly competitive and the McLarens were losing out – winning only four times. Prost drove well enough to win the Drivers' title for the second time in succession, but Williams took the Constructors', and the end was nigh. The 1987 season was the last for the TAG Turbos, and while the undaunted Prost still managed three race wins the car was looking less than it was.

Meanwhile in sports car racing, Porsche won its first Group C World Championship in 1982 with the 956, which was elected the motor sports car of the year. At Le Mans, the 956 factory Porsches stormed the field, with Ickx again taking the win with co-driver Derek Bell, as he had the previous year, and further Porsches finishing second through fifth. On the other side of the water, the Sebring 12 Hours was won by a Porsche 935. A year later, the new 934 took the Sebring crown, this time with privateer Americans Jim Mullen and Wayne Baker and Canadian Kees Nierop in the driving seat. It was a stunning victory for the little 934, and marked the middle of a thirteen-year unbeaten run by Porsche (1976–88), who hold almost all the records for this event with a total of seventeen wins to date.

This time Ickx and Bell missed out on the victory at Le Mans, but only just, with the sister car of Holbert, Haywood and Vern Schuppan just beating them to the line in a cloud of smoke as the engine blew up. Not to worry: that year Porsche extended its domination of the event to nine out of the top ten finishers; and repeated it the following year with Klaus Ludwig taking top honours. It was the start of a roll: in 1985 with the advent of the 962 and the remaining

Right The famous 'Jules No. 11' brings another Le Mans title to Porsche in 1981 in the hands of the great Jacky Ickx and Derek Bell.

956s still winning. Porsches made up eight of the top ten, and they merely swapped around for 86, with the 962s taking the first of two wins for the team of Bell, Holbert and Hans-Joachim Stuck. It was to be the last in the run, with Jaguar winning in 88, but by then Porsche had achieved a stunning seven in a row at the Sarthe circuit and won for ten of the last twelve years, often with Ickx as a part of the team.

It was Ickx who suggested to Porsche that the 959 would be ideally suited to the Paris–Dakar rally, which he'd already won for Mercedes. Taking this on board, in 1984 Porsche adapted a handful of 911s to 959 spec, entered, and won the great event, with René Metge and Antoine Lemoine piloting the eventual winner, although Ickx and co-driver Brasseur won several stages and finished a respectable sixth overall. The winning car was such a hybrid that records variously show it as a 911 4x4, an all-wheel-drive 911 Carrera 3.2, a 953 or a 911/59! It was the first sports car to take on the might of the off-roaders and win – and just to prove the point it followed it up by taking the Egyptian Rallye des Pharaohs some weeks later.

Above left Nikki Lauda pilots the Porsche-engined McLaren-TAG MP4/2 around Brands Hatch in 1984, for another win in his championship season.

Above The Porsche-designed, TAG-sponsored engine that powered the McLarens to victory in the mid 1980s.

Below The Joest-Porsche 956B of Klaus Ludwig, John Winter and Paulo Barilla wins at Le Mans in 1985, leading home an amazing eight Porsches in the top ten finishers.

Above *The Rothmans-liveried 959 stormed to victory in the 1984 Paris–Dakar and Pharaohs rallies.*

Below *Porsche developed this engine specifically for Indycar racing, using it in a March chassis in 1988. Sadly it never achieved what they'd hoped, and in 1990 they pulled out of the series.*

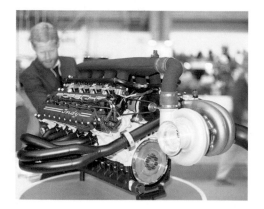

The following year the Porsches suffered technical problems, but by 1986 the 959s were back on top form and proved it with a one-two, Metge's car just beating Ickx's to take his second victory for Porsche, and his third overall.

With the Sarthe race a Porsche whitewash, the rallying events well under its belt and the Targa Florio no longer worth competing, and having no immediate Formula 1 prospects, Porsche briefly turned its attention to Indycar racing. In 1987 it unveiled the 2708 chassis, designed by Porsche engineers and built by the Munich firm of Messerschmitt Bolkow Blohm. The experienced Al Unser Senior was lead driver, but the car proved disappointing, so a year later Porsche switched to a March chassis and hired Teo Fabi to drive. The car scored one win at the Mid-Ohio event in 1989, but it was proving a costly and unproductive experiment. So at the end of 1990 Porsche stopped the programme, simultaneously announcing a return to Formula 1, planned to be in the form of a new V12 engine for the Arrows/Footwork team. This was to prove even more of a disaster, however, with the team dropping the engines mid-season, and since then Porsche seems to have accepted its inability to compete in these events and has concentrated on what it does best.

The 1990s

The Nineties opened in usual Porsche style, with a win at the Daytona 24 Hours (in a Porsche 962) for the team of John Winter, Pescarolo, Haywood and Wollek. But elsewhere the 962s weren't faring as well. Although every second car seemed to be a 962 in the WSC, they just couldn't seem to get past the top five, which were now dominated by Jaguar. Any number of teams were tweaking and poking them to little effect, and over the next couple of years they were gradually lost from the team sheet. Had there been a factory team things might have been different, but the early 1990s were some of the company's most fiscally difficult yet, and belts and budgets had to be tightened.

Meanwhile, there were rumblings of discontent among the various governing bodies of motor sport concerning the specifications of the Porsches that dominated Le Mans and similar events. It was history repeating itself – many times before the rules seemed to have been changed just when Porsche were getting the victories they deserved, and they had withdrawn from several such series in the past as a result. So this time they decided to set up a series specifically for Porsches, in which Porsche owners and drivers could compete head to head. It grabbed the imagination of racers and fans alike, and the resulting series, the Porsche Supercup and the Carrera Cup, have been a great success, often bringing forward potential Formula 1 and Le Mans drivers that might otherwise not have had the opportunity to race.

Le Mans, of course, continued to be a great haven for Porsche, both for the factory teams and the privateers. The 962 Dauer Porsche of Yanick Dalmas, Hurley Haywood and Mauro Baldini won, with a second entry finishing third, in 1994, and in 1996 Porsche once again managed the one-two-three, with the TWR Porsche of Alex Wurz (later in Formula 1), Davy Jones and Manuel Reuter taking the top spot, followed home by the factory-backed GT1s (see chapter 9 for a history of these two models). The GT1 later won three rounds of the BPR Global Endurance GT challenge, including Brands Hatch, with Thierry Boutsen and Stuck at the wheel, but they were allowed to enter only those three races with the GT1, and were excluded the following year when the BPR became the FIA GT championship. The Roock Porsche team of GT2s finished second overall at the end of the season, but they were again battling throughout with the indomitable McLaren F1.

The GT1s returned to Sarthe in 1997 but were again outwitted by the little TWR Porsche, now running for the Joest–Porsche team, driven by Michele Alboreto, Stefan Johansson and Tom Kristensen. A year later the factory GT1s finally took back their crown with a convincing one-two, the winning car being driven by Allan McNish (now with Toyota Formula 1), Laurent Aiello and Stephané Ortelli. Since then the Porsches have once again been pushed back down the field at their favourite event, winning the occasional class victory only, but no doubt their time will come again.

The GTs struggled at first in the new FIA GT championship, with even the McLarens now overtaken by the mighty Mercedes CLK, but by the end of the 1997 season the factory team cars of Dalmas/McNish and Wollek/Müller were pushing back up to take the lower podium

Below *The 1996 GT1 of Hans Stuck and Thierry Boutsen powers its way to a win at Brands Hatch in the BPR Global GT Challenge.*

places at Laguna Seca, while Bruno Eichmann's GT2 took second place in the overall GT2 title. The factory GT1s were permanent fixtures in second and third spot for most of the 1998 season with the GT1/98s, with a resulting second overall in the GT1 class, and it was looking hopeful for 1999 – only for Porsche to suffer another rule change that pushed the GT1s out, along with many of the other competitors, before the start of the season. The factory team packed up and deserted the series. The numerous privately-entered GT2s did their best, but the Chrysler Vipers swept to victory almost unchallenged in a very boring season. The private Freisinger Motorsport team finished third overall, but with some 23 points compared with Chrysler's 137 it wasn't a convincing result.

Above The 993-based 'Cup' car of Christophe Bouchot competing in the French Supercup series in 1995.

Below One of the Navision Porsche GT2s, developed by Roock Racing, leads its team-mate at Donnington in 1998.

The heritage continues

Going into the 21st century, Porsche was on the up. While still struggling against the McLaren and Jaguar beasts at the top of the endurance tables, the Audis in the rally events, and the Chryslers and Listers in the FIA GT, they were at least winning classes and a few points again. In the 2000 Le Mans, there was a GT class victory for Müller, Luhr and Wollek with the private Barbour-Porsche Team, and they finished thirteenth overall. The reliability of the Porsches was demonstrated when eight of the original fourteen entrants crossed the finishing line – a rather better ratio than usually expected. In the Sebring 12 Hour, now part of the American Le Mans series, Porsches once again completed a top three: Müller and Luhr won the GT category in their 911 GT3-R and claimed tenth overall, with second in the class going to American David Murry and Brit Johnny Mowlem from Skea Racing, and Haywood, Craig Stanton and Joel Reiser clinching third for their Reiser Callas Motorsport team. Again more than 50 per cent of the Porsches entered finished the race intact.

In the FIA GT series, the Freisinger Motorsport GT2 of Wolfgang Kaufmann and Wollek finished second at Monza, beating several of the invincible Chryslers in the process for the first time in two years. It was a turning point, and Kaufmann went on to score a third with Grasser at the A1-Ring before finally achieving victory in the Lausatzring 500km; he finished the season as seventh-placed driver. Suddenly Porsches were all over the points: the GT3-Rs had come into their own and were attacking the Vipers and Storms with alacrity. But it counted for

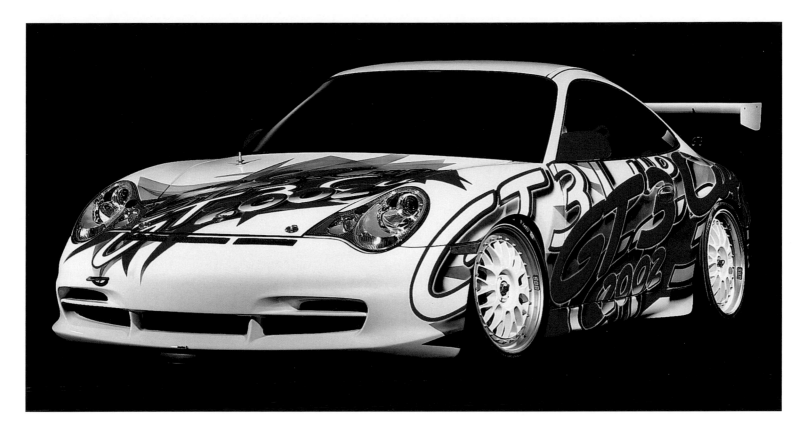

nothing other than a good spectacle – the GT3s were considered a separate class (the N-GTs) and any points they made were calculated for a different league table – which comprised *only* Porsche 911 GT3Rs, so was almost a new version of the Supercup. But there were certainly plenty of entrants.

The Porsche Pirelli Supercup continued – all-Porsche track racing with the ten rounds uniquely taking place immediately prior to ten of the Formula 1 events (the only GT racing series to do so), giving great exposure and experience to the drivers. Now in its tenth season, it is acknowledged as the world's fastest single-marque series and is proving a great training ground for future motorsport stars. Drivers compete in technically identical Porsche 911 GT3 Cup sports cars with 3.6-litre six-cylinder engines that produce 370bhp and 0–60mph in 4.2 seconds. The cars have an adjustable rear wing, front spoilers and side sills but otherwise are identical. Pirelli provides every vehicle with two sets of identical racing tyres per event. They compete in sprint races of approximately 43.5 miles (70 km).

Since 2001 a national Porsche Carrera Cup series has been run in Japan as support to the Japanese GT Championship. This follows the successful introduction of such series in Germany in 1989 and France in 1991. The races are basically sprints to the line, with each race taking approximately 30 minutes (depending on location). They are seen as proving ground for new drivers: Dirk Müller won the 1998 Carrera Cup as a UPS-Porsche junior, with team-mate Lucas Luhr repeating the result in 1999. Both received a Porsche works driver contract for 2000 to compete in the American Le Mans Series.

Meanwhile, the Boxsters and the revised 911s and 935s continue to race, across the world on-track and off-road; through deserts and snowfields, up mountains, in mud, streams and sand. The old models glide effortlessly around Goodwood and other historic meetings in the hands of the great and good, often raising the biggest cheers of the day and causing the most cameras to flash. They zip past you on the motorway in unofficial tag races. On the track or off, if you can name an event, a Porsche is probably competing in it right now.

Above *The 2002 911 GT3 Cup edition, race-bred for Supercup racing in Germany, France and Japan. Identical cars race in their own series, helping to prove the skill of individual drivers and support teams.*

MODEL DEVELOPMENT TIMELINES

The 356

Dimensions: Wheelbase 2100mm;
length between 3850mm (1950) and 4010mm
(1959); width 1660mm

1948–9: Gmünd coupés

The 356's direct predecessor, first produced in July
1948. The aluminium-bodied Gmünd coupés used
virtually all VW mechanicals from gearbox to
torsion bar suspension, and, of course, the Beetle-
derived engine. Drum brakes fitted all round.

1950: pre-A 356

Following the move to Stuttgart, the 356's integral
body was made of steel and the design given a
higher waistline than the Gmünd coupés and a
distinctive V-shaped roof to accommodate its split
screen. The 1.1-litre engine now produced 40bhp
and, along with the other engines on offer after
1952, was mated with Porsche's own gearbox.

1955–9: 356A

New engines, suspension altered. New curved
'V screen' did away with the need to split the

*Below Generations apart
but unmistakably the same
family: the first 356 (bottom)
poses alongside the 1998
911 Cabriolet.*

screen, vinyl replaced cloth inside. New dash,
combined ignition/starter. New gearbox in 1957.

1955: quad-cam Carreras

Launched at the 1955 Frankfurt Motor Show, these
engines were directly derived from racing
technology, with GT-denoted models aimed
specifically at motorsport. They were dry-sumped,
had reduced compression ratios and revved much
higher than the 356A. The cars around them were
lightweight, making them very potent on the road
for their day.

1959–63: 356B

A 90bhp 1600 engine was introduced for the Super
90, which got 'compensating rear springs' to
improve handling. Changes to bumper position,
headlamps and numerous interior details. 1961
saw numerous further changes, including twin
air intakes.

1963: 356C

Reworked engines, Super clutch on 75 and 95bhp
models, disc brakes introduced all round, rear
compensating spring special order only, no
external changes but rethink on interior details.

The 911

1963–7: Zero (0) Series, 1964–7 model year

Wheelbase 2,211mm; length 4,163mm; width
1,610mm. 911 (very briefly 901) first shown at
1963 Frankfurt Motor Show, goes on sale in
1964 with six-cylinder 2-litre engine. Targa
sales begin in very early 1967.

1967–8: A Series, 1968 model year

5.5in tyres introduced. The 911L has vented discs
from the 911S. Four-speed Sportomatic
introduced in 1967. Models available as Targa, rear
glass fixed as standard 1968.

1968–9: B Series, 1969 model year

Rear wheels moved 57mm further back to
enhance handling. Single battery replaced with
twin 35amp alternatives at the front in a bid to
keep the front end more securely planted and
thus enhance handling. S and E have mechanical

Bosch fuel injection. All models available as Targa.

1969–70: C Series, 1970 model year
4mm larger bore raises capacity to 2.2 litres. 225mm clutch introduced. Sportomatic no longer an option on 911S. Front upper strut attachment points moved forward 14mm. All available as Targa.

1970–71: D Series, 1971 model year
Significant developments: PVC-coated, galvanized underfloor areas introduced. All models available as Targa.

1971–2: E Series, 1972 model year
Engine stroke increased to 70.4mm giving 2.4-litre capacity. Compression ratio dropped to allow use of regular petrol. Gearbox uprated to cope with increased torque. External oil filler cap located between door and rear wheel. All models supplied with Fuchs wheels and available as Targa.

1972–3: F Series, 1973 model year
Wheelbase 2271mm; length 4127mm (RS 4147mm); width 1610mm. External oil filler removed due to customer confusion at the petrol pumps. Chin spoiler introduced on S to reduce front-end lift (option on T and E) and greater variance in standard wheels. Legendary Carrera 2.7 RS is first to be fitted with 'duck-tail' rear spoiler. All models, except RS, available as Targa.

1973–4: G Series, 1974 model year
Wheelbase 2271mm; length 4291mm; width 1610mm (Carrera 1652mm). Shock-absorbing bumpers introduced as a direct result of US legislation. Carrera comes with 'black look' trim. All models available as Targa.

1974–5: H Series, 1975 model year
Turbo introduced in early 1975 with four-speed gearbox but higher spec than the rest of the 911 range. 'Duck tail' replaced by 'whale tail' on Carrera models. Silver anniversary model launched, 1063 sold.

1975–6: I Series, 1976 model year
All 911 bodies completely zinc-coated, galvanized

steel. All models fitted with Bosch K-Jetronic. Sportomatic becomes a three- rather than four-speed option.

1976–7: J Series, 1977 model year
Wheelbase 2271mm; length 4291mm (Turbo 4318mm); width 1610mm (Carrera 3.0 1652mm, Turbo 1829mm). Sportomatic cars get brake servo assistance. 'Black look' trim standard on Targas.

**1977–9: K and L Series (the SC),
1978–9 model year**
Super Carrera combines old 911 and Carrera with 3-litre engine, all fitted with servo-assisted brakes. Turbo receives larger engine equipped with intercooler, and 'tea-tray' spoiler replaces 'whale tail'.

1979–80: SC (new A Series), 1980 model year
Revised ignition and camshaft timing gives SC 188bhp. Turbo gets twin exit exhaust.

1980–81: SC (new B Series), 1981 model year
Significant developments. First year of Porsche's use of seventeen-digit international chassis serial number. SC now runs on 98 RON.

1981–2: SC (new C Series), 1982 model year
Limited-edition 'Ferry Porsche' goes on sale. 'Tea-tray' spoiler option for SC.

1982–3: SC (new D Series), 1983 model year
Cabriolet rushed into production and launched following successful design study.

1983–4: Carrera (new E Series), 1984 model year
Wheelbase 2271mm; length 4291mm (Turbo 4318mm); width 1610mm (Turbo and Turbo-look 1829mm). Carrera replaces the SC. Bore and stroke increases raise capacity to 3164cc, Digital Motor Electronic engine management and engine oil-fed chain tensioner introduced. Turbo-look option available for 911, which not only makes car slower by adding 50kg to its weight, but also increases the drag created by the wider body (track 1432mm front/1500mm rear).

1984–5: Carrera (new F Series), 1985 model year
Significant developments: Carrera engine

available with catalytic converter and lower compression giving 207bhp. Four-spoke steering wheel standard across the range. Turbo-look option available for 911.

1985–6: Carrera (new G Series), 1986 model year
Sport seats no-cost option. Turbo-look track 1434mm front/1526mm rear.

1986–7: Carrera (new H Series), 1987 model year
Turbo available as a Targa and Cabriolet for the first time. Slat-nose becomes an option. 915 transmission replaced by Getrag-built G50. Power hood standard on Cabriolet.

1987–8: Carrera (new J Series), 1988 model year
Celebration anniversary model available. Club Sport model introduced weighing 50kg less. Blueprinted engine pushes power to around 241bhp.

1988–9: Carrera (new K Series), 1989 model year
16in wheels now standard. Speedster introduced and available with either the Turbo-look or the race-derived flat-nose bodies.

1988–9: 964, 1989 model year
Wheelbase 2271 mm; length 4250mm; width 1651mm. Launched in January 1989 with new engine, suspension, brakes and numerous body parts. Porsche claim the 964 shares only 13 per cent of its parts with its predecessors. Carrera 4 split torque 31/69 front to rear. All-wheel ABS and power steering standard, catalyst introduced.

1989–90: 964, 1990 model year
All pre-964 models now deleted. Carrera 2 introduced, Targa and Cabriolet available for both C2 and C4 models. Tiptronic available on C2.

1990–91: 964, 1991 model year
Rear-drive 320bhp 964 Turbo introduced.

1991–2: 964, 1992 model year
Stripped-out Carrera 2 RS introduced. 381bhp Turbo S model available to order (80 built).

1992–3: 964, 1993 model year
Speedster introduced. 3.6 Turbo production begins in January 1993.

1993–4: 993, 1994 model year
Wheelbase 2272mm; length 4245mm; width 1735mm (Carrera 4S and Turbo 1795mm). 993 production begins in January 1994. Internal engine upgrades increase power. Multi-link rear suspension across the range. Four-pot brakes standard front and rear.

1994–5: 993, 1995 model year
Carrera RS introduced. Redesigned all-wheel-drive system on C4. Tiptronic S first appears. Four-wheel-drive Turbo with twin turbochargers and six-speed gearbox introduced.

1995–6: 993, 1996 model year
VarioCam engines give more power. Sliding glass-roofed Targa introduced.

1996–7: 993, 1997 model year
430bhp Turbo S offered as ultimate 993 run-out limited-edition model.

1997–8: 993, 1998 model year
Production of all-wheel drive and Turbo continues until July 1998.

The 912

1965:
Replacement for 356 is launched. Visually identical to the new 911, the 912 not only shares the 911's body, but its chassis too. Brakes and four-cylinder air-cooled engine are carried over from 356, however.

1969:
912 gets longer wheelbase and revised body of current 911 model, but all production ends soon after.

1975:
912 reintroduced for one year, fitted with 2-litre VW four-cylinder from defunct 914. Model is stop-gap until all-new, front-engined, water-cooled coupé is introduced.

The 914

1969:

The 914 is launched as a replacement for the 912, with a choice of either a fuel-injected 1.7-litre flat-four or a carburettor-fed 911-sourced 2-litre six-cylinder, producing 80bhp and 110bhp respectively.

1973:

The six-cylinder 914/6 is dropped from the model line and replaced by a new 2-litre four-cylinder engine. Mahle and Fuchs alloy wheels are available as optional extras on all four-cylinder cars.

1974:

Original 1.7-litre four-cylinder engine is enlarged to 1.8 litres and given a new Bosch L-Jetronic injection system, but power is down to 76bhp because of US emission regulations. European models had twin Weber downdraught carburettors fitted in lieu and produced 85bhp.

1976:

914 production ends.

The racing models

1948: 356 (001)

1951: 356/2 SL Gmünd Coupé

1953–54: 356 1500 S & Super

1953–55: 550 Spyder and Spyder Coupé

1956–58: 550A Spyder RS

1957: 356 Speedster Carrera

1957–60: 718 RSK (F2)

1958–60: 718 RSK Spyder

1960: 718 RS60

1960–62: 356 B Abarth-Carrera GT

1961: 718 RS61

1961–62: Monoposto F2 (718)

1961–63: 718 RS61 Coupé

1961–64: 718 RS61 W-RS Spyder

1962: 804 Formula 1

Above *A line-up of the models available from Porsche in 1980s.*

1964–65: 904 Carrera GTS Coupé

1965: 904/6 and 904/8

1966–67: Carrera 6 (906) Short Tail and Long Tail

1967: 910 Coupé (Carrera 6) and Spyder

1967–68: 907 Short Tail and Long Tail

1968–69: 908 Coupé Short Tail and Long Tail, 908/02 Spyder (909)

1968–70: 911 (Rally)

1969: 917 Long Tail

1970–71: 917K Short Tail

1970–75: 908/03 Spyder

1971: 917/20 Long Tail

1971–73: 917/10 (CanAm)

1972–74: 917/30 (CanAm)

1972–75: RS / RSR Turbo-Carrera (911)

1975–1976: 908/04 Spyder

1976: 935 and 936

1976–77: 934 / 930 (911)

1977: 935/77 and 935-02 'Baby'

1977–78: 936/77

1978: 935/78 'Moby Dick'

1978–80: 936/78

1979–84: 935 K3 (Kremer), 911 (Rally)

1980: 924 Carrera GT

1981: 936/81

1982: 935 K4 (Kremer)

1982–87: 956 / 956 B

1983–88: 962

1984: 911 Carrera 4x4 (Dakar Rally)

1985–93: 962 C

1986: 959 (Dakar Rally)

1988–89: 944 Turbo Cup

1988–93: 962 CK6 (Kremer)

1990–97: 911 Carrera Cup / Super Cup

1993: 911 Turbo GT / Turbo S (964)

1994: Dauer-962 GT LM

1995–97: TWR WSC-95 (Joest)

1996: 911 GT1

1997: 911 GT1 Evo

1998: LMP1-98 (WSC-95)

1998: 911 GT1-98

1998–2001: 911 GT3 Cup (996)

1999–2001: 911 GT2 (996)

Below *Three from 1998: (from back) the 911 Coupé, Boxster, and 911 Cabriolet.*